RATIONAL LIVING

SOME PRACTICAL INFERENCES
FROM MODERN PSYCHOLOGY

BY

HENRY CHURCHILL KING

PRESIDENT OF OBERLIN COLLEGE
AUTHOR OF "RECONSTRUCTION IN THEOLOGY," "THEOLOGY AND THE
SOCIAL CONSCIOUSNESS," "PERSONAL AND IDEAL ELEMENTS
IN EDUCATION," ETC.

The Chautauqua Press
CHAUTAUQUA, NEW YORK
MCMVI

COPYRIGHT, 1905,
BY THE MACMILLAN COMPANY.

Set up and electrotyped. Published September, 1905. Reprinted December, 1905; March, 1906; April, 1906.

PREFACE

It is with considerable hesitancy that one undertakes to point out the practical suggestions of modern psychological investigations. Scientific workers in this field have a natural prejudice against attempts to make their science quickly useful; and this feeling is so strong on the part of many, that one almost seems to proclaim himself to such as a charlatan at once, if he attempts to draw practical inferences from this study, and to make these inferences generally available. But is it not possible that we might well heed just here Hilty's illuminating word? "Truth, wherever it may be sought, is, as a rule, so simple that it often does not look learned enough."

It is true that the full significance of the inferences will hardly be felt apart from a reasonable presentation of their psychological grounds; and it is also true that many attempts so practically to use psychological results have been fanciful and extravagant, and have tended to lay extreme emphasis upon the least assured results of recent investigations. Still, it were extraordinary if such extended and thorough study of human nature as the recent years have shown had no valuable suggestions for living, that all men would do well to heed; and James and Sully and Baldwin and Royce—to mention no others—have certainly left us no room for doubt upon that point. And it ought not to be impossible to present the psychological facts, even in somewhat popular form, with sufficient accuracy and fullness to give weight and point to the practical suggestions involved, provided these practical inferences are drawn with sanity and moderation, and from assured results. And it is only with such inferences that this book intends to deal. It makes no appeal to the mere love of novelty or mystery. It intends to build soberly upon the whole broad range of psychological investigation.

If I may be allowed frankly to express in these introductory words my personal feeling and conviction, I should say that I have not been able to doubt the seriousness and value of the counsels lying back of this modern psychological study. Even where the counsel is not new, it comes with fresh force, when its psychological justification can be clearly shown. Manifold as, no doubt, the shortcomings of this book are, it is still no hasty compilation, but embodies those suggestions which, through a number of years, have appealed both to myself and to many others as of interest and importance. I have found myself using so often, in practical counsel and in ethical and theological inquiry, the psychological principles here appealed to, that it has seemed reasonable to hope that the book might have some real service to render to others. For it is but too obvious, on the one hand, that many students complete their courses in psychology with but small sense of its direct bearing on life, and so fail to grasp its real significance, through the very lack of application of its principles; and, on the other hand, that men generally need, and are able intelligently to receive, much of the best that psychology has to give, but that it is difficult to find in any fullness except in more or less technical treatises. There seemed, therefore, to be a place and a need for the attempt here made.

While, then, the book does not aim to

be a technical treatise upon psychology, nor profess to embody the results of *original* psychological investigation, it does distinctly aim to make generally available the most valuable suggestions for living that can be drawn from the results of the best workers in this field. I have, consequently, quoted freely and sometimes at length, both to give the reader immediate access to the original authority for the psychological facts, and to give him opportunity to judge of the justness of the inference drawn in any given case. For I, of course, do not mean to hold those from whom I quote responsible for all my inferences, though I have meant that these should be reached with scrupulous care.

The very plan of the book makes my indebtedness to others very large—an indebtedness which I have intended to recognize in each case by specific reference.

At the same time, it is hoped that the book does not lack the original suggestiveness and the unity that should give added significance to the individual suggestions. The grouping of the material, and some of the indicated ethical, religious, and generally practical applications and implications of psychological principles, it is hoped, may not be without interest even to those who have given considerable attention to psychological study. The discussion aims to give in the field of practical living something of that sense of unity and sureness that the investigator in natural science has, and that can come only from a knowledge of the *laws* involved. In this aim it joins hands with all those writings — much more numerous of late — that have sought to give to both ethics and religion a true psychological basis.

The material is gathered under four great and closely interwoven inferences from modern psychology. These constitute the four main divisions of the book. Under each division an attempt is made to give briefly but sufficiently the psychological basis, and then to point out the most important derived practical suggestions. Even in the statement of the psychological facts, however, it will be seen—in order to save repetition—the practical has not been entirely excluded. The title of the book, thus, grows directly out of its precise aims.

At the same time, it has not seemed wise to exclude all consideration of the broader philosophical bearings of the discussions; and at certain points their consideration has seemed almost required for a really satisfactory result, especially in parts of the last two divisions of the book. These parts are necessarily somewhat more difficult reading; but they will be readily recognized, and may be, perhaps, well enough omitted by those who are seeking only practical results. For the more philosophically inclined, it is hoped that these brief philosophical digressions may add somewhat to the value and suggestiveness of the book.

HENRY CHURCHILL KING.

Oberlin College, June, 1905.

CONTENTS

INTRODUCTION

THE FOUR GREAT INFERENCES FROM MODERN PSYCHOLOGY . . 1

THE COMPLEXITY OF LIFE: THE MULTIPLICITY AND INTRICACY OF RELATIONS

INTRODUCTION

NOT CONFUSION, BUT GREATER RICHNESS 5

CHAPTER I

THE PSYCHOLOGICAL GROUNDS FOR THE RECOGNITION OF THE COMPLEXITY OF LIFE 7
  I. The Evidence of the Different Departments of Psychology 7
    1. Physiological Psychology 7
    2. Race Psychology 7
    3. Pathological Psychology 7
    4. Comparative Psychology 8
    5. Experimental Method in 8
  II. The Need of a Wide Range of Interests 9
  III. The Relatedness of All 14
    1. Recognition of Relatedness of All 14
    2. Human Nature Avenges Itself for Disregard of the Range of Its Interests 15
    3. The Denial of the Possible Separation of the Sacred and the Secular 17
    4. Absorption in the Lower Defeats Itself 20

CONTENTS

CHAPTER II

RECOGNITION OF THE PARADOXES OF LIFE — OPPOSING RELATIONS 22
  I. The All-Inclusive Paradox of Ends and Means 22
  II. The Paradoxes of the Different Spheres of Life 23
   1. Paradoxes in the Physical Life 23
   2. Paradoxes in the Intellectual Life 24
   3. Paradoxes in the Moral Life 26
   4. Paradoxes in the Religious Life 31
   5. Choosing One's Lifework and Abiding Character — The "Hierarchy of *Mes*" 31
   6. The Fundamental Paradox of Life. Docility and Initiative 32

CHAPTER III

THE EMPHASIS OF PSYCHOLOGY ON CONDITIONS 39
  I. The Lessons of Natural Science 40
  II. The Significance of Common Work and Duties 42
  III. No Magical Inheritance 44
  IV. No Conditions in General 45

THE UNITY OF MAN

CHAPTER IV

THE UNITY OF MIND AND BODY — INTRODUCTION 47
  I. Ascetic Treatment of Bodily Conditions 47
  II. Not a Materialistic Position 49

CHAPTER V

THE UNITY OF MIND AND BODY — THE PSYCHOLOGICAL EVIDENCE 55
  I. The Law of Diffusion 55

CONTENTS

	PAGE
II. Psychical Effects of Bodily Training	57
III. The Close Connection of the Will and Muscular Activity	58
IV. The Physical Basis of Habit	61
V. The Evidence of Hypnotism	63

CHAPTER VI

THE UNITY OF MIND AND BODY — SUGGESTIONS FOR LIVING . . 64
- I. The Body Influences the Mind 64
  - 1. The Need of Well-Oxygenated Blood 64
  - 2. The Need of Surplus Nervous Energy. Effects of Fatigue 67
    - (1) The Effects of Fatigue on Attention and Self-Control 67
    - (2) Direct Effect of Fatigue on Nerve Conditions 70
    - (3) The Consequent Effects of Fatigue on All Perceptions and Activities 71
    - (4) The Need of Physical Training 77
- II. The Influence of Mind on Body 78
  - 1. Power of Self-Control Even in the Insane 79
  - 2. The Will in Determining Conditions of Health . . 80
    - (1) In Achieving Rest 80
    - (2) In Avoiding Hurry 81
    - (3) In Meeting the Special Conditions of Surplus Nervous Energy 82
    - (4) In Control of the Emotions 82
  - 3. Self-Control Positive, not Negative 83
- III. Mutual Influence of Body and Mind — Habits 85
  - 1. The Significance of Habit for Mental Life 86
  - 2. Opportunities for Will Training in Formation of Habits in Education 88
  - 3. James' Maxims on Habit 90
    - (1) Launch Yourself with Decided Initiative . . 91
    - (2) Allow no Exceptions 91
    - (3) Seize the First Opportunity to Act 92
    - (4) Gratuitous Exercise of Effort 92

CONTENTS

	PAGE
IV. The True Place of Asceticism	93
1. The Body not Evil *per se*	94
2. Asceticism, As Negative, No Full Goal of Life	95
3. Not Two Kinds of Christianity	96
4. The True Asceticism	99

CHAPTER VII

THE UNITY OF THE MIND — THE PSYCHOLOGICAL EVIDENCE	103
I. Interdependence of All Intellectual Functions	103
II. Interdependence of Intellect, Feeling, and Will	106
III. Trend Toward the Denial of Abstract Elements in the Mind	108
IV. The Mind's Constant Search for Unity	108

CHAPTER VIII

THE UNITY OF THE MIND — SUGGESTIONS FOR LIVING	111
I. The Intellectual Conditions	113
1. Intellectual Helps	113
(1) A Wide Circle of Permanent Interests	114
(2) Knowledge of Oneself	114
(3) Discernment of What Moral Progress Is	118
(4) Particularly, Clearness and Definiteness in Memory, Imagination, and Thinking	120
2. Intellectual Hindrances	124
(1) Premature Multiplication of Many Points of View. "Truth-hunting"	124
(2) "Over-sophistication"	127
(3) Making Insights Take the Place of Doing	128
(4) Intellectual Vagueness	130
(5) Dangers in Habits of Study	133
II. Emotional Conditions	135
1. The Stimulating Effect of Joyful Emotions	135
2. The Danger of Strained and Sham Emotions	138
3. The Influence of Moods on Willing	140
4. The Danger of Passive Emotion	141
5. The Need of Power to Withstand Strong Emotion	142

THE CENTRAL IMPORTANCE OF WILL AND ACTION

CHAPTER IX

	PAGE
THE CENTRAL IMPORTANCE OF WILL AND ACTION — THE PSYCHOLOGICAL EVIDENCE	145
I. The Suggestion of Evolution	146
II. Impulse to Action, Fundamental	146
III. The Natural Terminus of Every Experience is Action	149
1. The Body Organized for Action	149
(1) The Circulation of the Blood	149
(2) The Nervous System	150
(3) The Muscular System	150
(4) In the Human Body as a Whole	152
2. The Mind Organized for Action	153
IV. For the Very Sake of Thought and Feeling, One Must Act	154
V. The Will in Attention	159
VI. The Preëminent Influence of Practical Interests in All Consciousness	161
1. In Conceiving and Naming Things	162
2. In Reasoning	163
3. In Our Philosophical Solutions	163
(1) Influence of Practical Interests	163
(2) Philosophy Depends on Practical Considerations	165
(3) Convictions Must be Wrought out in Action	165
4. Using One's Powers	166
VII. Some Current Psychological Emphases	171

CHAPTER X

THE CENTRAL IMPORTANCE OF WILL AND ACTION — SUGGESTIONS FOR LIVING	176
I. The Enormous Place of Will and Action in Life	176
II. The Fundamental Character of Self-Control	180
1. Self-Control Fundamental to a Moral and Religious Character	180

CONTENTS

		PAGE
2. Self-Control Fundamental to Happiness		182
3. Self-Control Fundamental to Influence		185
4. Self-Control Positive, not Negative		186
(1) Object Must Continually Change for Us		191
(2) The Possession of a Large Circle of Interests		191
(3) Persistent Staying in the Presence of the Best		192
III. Objectivity a Prime Condition of Character, and Happiness, and Influence		192
IV. Work a Chief Means to Character, and Happiness, and Influence		198

THE CONCRETENESS OF THE REAL — THE INTER-RELATEDNESS OF ALL

CHAPTER XI

THE CONCRETENESS OF THE REAL — THE PSYCHOLOGICAL EVIDENCE, CONFIRMED BY THE HISTORY OF THOUGHT . . 210

I. The General Trend in Psychology Toward Recognition of this Concreteness 210
II. The Mind Made for Relations 213
III. One Reason for the Place and Power of Art and Literature 214
IV. The Influence of the Idea of the Organism in the History of Thought 215
    1. The Idea of the Organism Before Hegel 216
    2. The Idea of the Organism in Hegel 216
    3. The Idea of the Organism Since Hegel 218
V. A New Protest Constantly Needed in the Interest of the Whole Man 220
    1. The Protest in the History of Literature 222
    2. The Protest in Philosophy 223
    3. The Protest in History 224
    4. The Protest in Education 227
VI. The Emphasis on Persons and Personal Relations — The Social Self 228
    1. The Human Body Looks to Personal Association . 229

CONTENTS

		PAGE
2.	The Witness of Infancy	230
3.	The Witness of the Moral History of the Race	231
4.	The Witness of Philosophy	232
5.	The Whole Man, Revealed only in Personal Relations	233

CHAPTER XII

THE CONCRETENESS OF THE REAL — SUGGESTIONS FOR LIVING . 236

I. Respect for the Liberty and the Personality of Others . 236
   1. Recognition of the Moral Freedom of Others . . . 236
   2. Recognition of the Sacredness of the Person 239
      (1) Every Person is an End in Himself 239
      (2) A Prime Condition in All Friendship 244
      (3) A Test of Moral Progress 245
II. The Power of Personal Association 246
   1. Influence of Imitation 246
   2. One Must be Won to Character 247
   3. We are Made for Personal Relations 248
   4. One Cannot Learn to Love Alone 249
   5. Personal Association the Greatest Means 249

RATIONAL LIVING

INTRODUCTION

THE FOUR GREAT INFERENCES FROM MODERN PSYCHOLOGY

ONE of the marked characteristics of this realistic age of ours is the enormous amount of investigation that has been given in the last thirty years to empirical psychology. Wundt's epoch-making *Outlines of Physiological Psychology* was published as late as 1874, and his Leipsic psychological laboratory—the first in the world—was not founded until 1879. No other department of study directly connected with philosophy has had anything like equal attention, or made anything like equal growth. And in no other department has America had so noteworthy a share, as the literature of the subject clearly shows. Such extended and thorough-going study of the nature of man, ought certainly to have some meaning for practical living. It concerns, therefore, every intelligent man to ask what the significance of this movement is.

It should be remembered from the beginning, however, that, although modern psychology has been specially characterized by emphasis upon the physiological and experimental sides, these lines of investigation by no means exhaust the meaning of this later psychological movement. For, as Royce says, "One must insist that the study of neurological facts has, although very great, still only relative value for the psychologist. For one thing, what the psychologist wants to understand is mental life, and to this end he uses all his other facts only as means; and, for the rest, *any physical expression of mental life* which we can learn to interpret becomes as genuinely interesting to the psychologist as does a brain function."[1]

The experimental method, too, it should be noted, is no attack on the methods previously employed. Most sober psychologists would agree with Külpe — himself a most able worker in experimental psychology — that "experiment can no more take the place of introspection in psychology than it can that of observation in physics. It is only able, as

[1] *Outlines of Psychology*, p. 12.

it is only intended, to supplement the previous method by filling the gaps which remain when introspection is employed alone, by checking its descriptions, and by making it generally more reliable."[1]

Using the term modern psychology, then, to cover the trend of all later psychological investigations, and not merely those of experimental or physiological psychology, what are the most important inferences from modern psychology? What does it mean?

The answer can be given very compactly. There seem to the writer to be four great inferences from modern psychology, and each with suggestions for life and character — that is, with direct suggestion of the conditions of growth, of character, of happiness, and of influence. These four inferences are: Life is complex; man is a unity; will and action are of central importance; and the real is concrete. In other words, modern psychology has four great emphases; for it may be said to urge upon us the recognition of the multiplicity and intricacy of the relations everywhere confronting us; of the essential unity of the relations involved in our own nature; of the fact that this

[1] *Outlines of Psychology*, p. 10.

unity demands action and is best expressed in action; and that we are, thus, everywhere shut out from resting in abstractions and must find reality only in the concrete. Manifestly these contentions are all closely interwoven, and they may even be regarded as all summed up in the last — as asserting the inter-relatedness of all.

For if only the concrete is real, then life is, in the first place, no abstraction or series of abstractions, but rich and complex beyond all formulation. In this complexity, secondly, no sharp lines can be drawn, all is interwoven; the life of man, therefore, is a unity — body and mind. But all experiences, bodily and mental, tend to terminate in action, in which alone the whole man is seen; will and action, then, are of central importance. The four propositions tend thus to fall together. It is these four propositions which form the subjects of the main divisions of our entire inquiry.

THE COMPLEXITY OF LIFE: THE MULTIPLICITY AND INTRICACY OF RELATIONS

INTRODUCTION

NOT CONFUSION, BUT GREATER RICHNESS

PSYCHOLOGY'S first emphasis is naturally upon the complexity of life — the multiplicity and intricacy of the relations everywhere confronting us. For the first effect of the study of this later psychology, it must be confessed, is likely to prove confusing and even bewildering; the old familiar landmarks seem all gone. There are no sharp distinctions, no hard and fast classifications, no short and simple formulas.

The old way in which, without hesitation or misgiving, we built up the structure of our mental life — combining simple atomic sensations into perceptions, perceptions into conceptions, conceptions into judgments, and judgments into syllogisms — is suddenly closed for us. We are forced to question the truth of such a process at every stage. As we face the facts of modern psychological investigation, it is not the simple, the direct, the abstract, that we see, but the necessity rather for what James calls "the reinstatement of the vague and inarticulate to its proper place in our mental life."[1] It is characteristic, indeed, of the modern point of view that James should begin his psychological inquiry, not with assumed simple sensations, but with the attempt to point out only the chief characters of the whole concrete stream of consciousness.[2] The problem *is* complex and intricate. Life seems to have overflowed its banks, and we wonder if it can ever be brought under rule again.

But we need not resist this trend of the newer psychology. For it is only the refusal to make the formulation of life simple by ignoring many of its facts. It does not mean final confusion, but only greater richness. Indeed, it may be doubted if there is anything that the health of the whole life — physical, intellectual, and spiritual — needs more, or more continuously, than a strong conviction of the complexity of life. We may well heed, therefore, this insistence of modern psychology.

[1] *Psychology*, Vol. I, p. 254.
[2] *Psychology*, Vol. I, Chap. IX; Ctr. Külpe, *op. cit.*, p. 22.

CHAPTER I

THE PSYCHOLOGICAL GROUNDS FOR THE RECOGNITION OF THE COMPLEXITY OF LIFE

I. THE EVIDENCE OF THE DIFFERENT DEPARTMENTS OF PSYCHOLOGY

EVERY one of the departments of psychological investigation serves to emphasize this complexity. Even in the field of the older psychology—the study of the normal mind of the adult civilized man—it is now recognized that the facts are far less simple than they at first seemed. The immense emphasis now laid on the accurate study of the simpler phenomena of *child life*—itself seen to have wonderful variety—is evidence of this felt complexity. *Physiological psychology* emphasizes the complex intertwining at every point of the physical and the psychical, especially the correlation of psychical with brain processes. *Race psychology* adds the study of national traits, and of the relations of all minds, civilized and barbarous. *Pathological psychology* affirms the essential unity of normal and abnormal minds, that insanity itself only carries to extremes tendencies which lie in us all. *Comparative psychology* goes a step farther and calls attention to the many likenesses between human and animal minds. Finally the felt need in psychology of the *experimental method* that has so largely characterized the recent advances in the subject, is itself a further recognition of the complexity of the psychical phenomena.

It is not strange, then, that the results of such varied investigations, every one of which has something vital to contribute to the understanding of this enigma of our life, should, at first sight, seem bewildering. "What is man?" It is this question, in all its complexity of meaning, that modern psychology seeks to answer.

And modern philosophy confirms, here, the psychological trend. For man, Erdmann says, is the great subject of modern philosophy—but man in all the fullness of his concrete existence; man, body and spirit; man, intellect, feeling, and will; man, as world in little and God in little; man, as summing up all in a complexity of being, rich past tracing out. For modern philosophy begins, like the Reformation it reflects, in protest — protest against the narrowing of the interests of man, protest against the separation of sacred and secular, protest against the denial of legitimate worldly interests; and among all the heresies of the age it counts none so great as the heresy of denying the complexity of the life of man, and of removing from religion the most of life.

II. THE NEED OF A WIDE RANGE OF INTERESTS

Psychology speaks here with no uncertain sound. It knows well that a *man's world* is no greater than the number of objects to which he can attend with interest; this is his world — the only world in which he really lives. He moves among many other things, but so far as they are ignored, they practically do not exist for him. Psychology knows, too, that the meaning of *experience*, itself, is what we attend to; that the environment that really makes us is not, as is so often said, all that surrounds us, but only those parts of our surroundings to which we *attend;* that a man's life is measured, therefore, by the interests to which he can respond; and that his growth depends on the enlarging of this circle of interests. So James says: "A man's empirical thought depends on the things he has experienced, but what these shall be is to a large extent determined by his habits of attention. A thing may be present to him a thousand times, but, if he persistently fails to notice it, it cannot be said to enter into his experience. We are all seeing flies, moths, and beetles by the thousand, but to whom, save an entomologist, do they say anything distinct? On the other hand, a thing met only once in a lifetime may leave an indelible experience in the memory. Let four men make a tour in Europe. One will bring home only picturesque impressions—costumes and colors, parks and views and works of architecture, pictures and statues. To another all this will be non-existent; and distances and prices, populations and drainage-arrangements, door- and window-fastenings, and other useful statistics will take their place. A third will give a rich account of the theaters, restaurants, and public balls, and naught besides; whilst the fourth will perhaps have been so wrapped in his own subjective broodings as to tell little more than a few names of places through which he passed. Each has selected out of the same mass of presented objects those which suited his private interest, and has made his experience thereby."[1]

Moreover, one's possible *influence* over others depends, in no small degree, upon the range of his interests; for influence normally requires sympathetic understanding, and sympathetic understanding means the ability to enter into the interests of the other man — to see the matter from his point of view. Here lies a main task of every teacher, and of every leader of men, who does not mean to be a mere demagogue. If one cares to exert the highest influence, then, — not merely to dominate another's choices — he must seek such an influence as the other shall be able to recognize as simply the demand of his own sanest and best self. That influence is possible only to the man who has sufficient breadth of interests to enter into another's life with understanding, respect, and sympathy.

For breadth and depth of influence, one needs especially to be always attuned to the "ever-recurring fundamental characteristics of human life" — the common, simple, large,

[1] *Psychology*, Vol. I, pp. 286-287.

and deep interests of the race. Only so can one carry something of the appeal made, for example, by a great work of art. And the highly educated man needs to be carefully on his guard just here. He must not become a mere member of a clique.

Psychology knows, moreover, that whatever *freedom* a man possesses—the condition of the very possibility of character—depends on his having more than one interest to which he can attend. Moral victory requires the power to attend to something else than the temptation which threatens completely to engross one. It is often, thus, a vital matter, for the very sake of one's freedom, that he should have more than one absorbing interest.

Even *sanity* requires a reasonable breadth of interests. Peary has borne witness out of his long Arctic experience, that the educated man, even if other things were not wholly equal, showed greater capacity than the uneducated for endurance of the privation and hardship of Arctic exploration and the Arctic night, for the very reason that he had more things in which he could be interested. One of the chief marks of insanity, indeed, is the all-absorbing, single "insistent idea."

A "store of permanent and valuable interests" is, therefore, both a sign and a guard of sanity.

For all these reasons psychology knows that the acquisition of a considerable number of permanent and valuable interests is one of the prime objects of education, and one of the main factors in a "reasonable character." A chief test of one's education, therefore, is the question whether it has awakened in one's mind some permanent and valuable interests. So Sully says: "The teacher should regard it as an important part of the training of the attention to arouse interest, to deepen and fix it in certain definite directions, and gradually to enlarge its range. Volkmann remarks that the older pedagogic had as its rule: 'Make your instruction interesting'; whereas, the newer has the precept, 'Instruct in such a way that an interest may awake and remain active for life'."[1] A similar aim every thoughtful man must have in mind in his own self-training. And it needs hardly to be pointed out how imperative is *time* in the building up of a wide range of interests. As Royce says: "It is the leisurely traveler who finds time to cultivate new

[1] *Outlines of Psychology*, p. 105.

habits, and thus gradually to see the wonders as they are."[1]

III. THE RELATEDNESS OF ALL

Psychology's emphasis upon the complexity of life—the multiplicity and intricacy of the relations involved—implies the recognition of the relatedness of all, and so suggests at once that the degree in which any interest exists for us depends upon the degree in which we have brought it into connection with the rest of life. We are awake to the full significance of any idea only when we see it in all its varied bearings. There are, thus, widely different *"degrees of wakefulness"* to even the highest interests. When one feels the difference between a dead and a live truth—a truth that he took by rote and the same truth born again within him,—he may well wonder if he were wholly awake before. To feel the same thing continuously, Hobbes long ago saw, is practically to feel nothing at all. "A completely uniform and unchanged condition," says Höffding, "has a tendency to arrest consciousness."[2]

[1] *Outlines of Psychology*, p. 228.
[2] *Outlines of Psychology*, p. 45.

So Lotze says: "By attention we gain something merely in case the content mentally represented gives occasion for its work to our *relating and comparing* faculty of knowledge. Even an altogether simple content is at least compared by us with other simple contents, or with itself at different moments of its duration. If we disregard this fact, then the mere persistence of the content, with whatever intensity it may occur, is of absolutely no help to us. It is understood, finally, that this relating of one content to another can be carried further at pleasure. We can therefore certainly distinguish yet other different degrees of consciousness concerning the content of an idea;—and this according as we mentally represent the idea itself and its own nature, or its connection with other ideas, or, finally, its value and significance for the totality of our personal life."[1] Only in the last case does the idea or interest have for us its full value; and this evidently requires the completest recognition of the relatedness of all.

It is, indeed, not too much to say, that *human nature everywhere avenges itself for any lack of reasonable regard for the wide range of its interests*. Many illustrations will suggest

[1] *Outlines of Psychology*, pp. 45-46.

themselves. The Cavalier needs the correction of the Puritan; and the Puritan the correction of the Cavalier. Oberlin couldn't paint all its buildings red in the early days, though it was proved conclusively that red was the cheapest and most durable paint, and therefore ought to be used; human nature was too much for it. It is a genuine touch of nature that makes Mrs. Ward's Marcella rightly but illogically retain a rich rug for her bare lodging, even when she has left all the world behind for her work among the poor. The lack of a sense of humor has turned many a wise man into a fool. The conscientious denial by a man of the value of the beautiful has more than once wrought disastrously in the character of his children. The endeavor rigorously to rule out the simply recreative has, in whole lives and generations, brought speedy punishment. The attempt to annihilate the physical in him has, for many a monk of the desert, kept his attention fixed the more fatally on the physical. The distrust of truth in all but one direction has made possible for the Church its not wholly creditable history in relation to science. This exclusive attitude is nowhere justified.

And one can hardly fail to see that this recognition of the relatedness of all necessarily carries with it a *denial of the possible separation of the sacred and the secular*. What has already been said concerning the need of a wide range of interests shows that the very constitution of the mind demands, for the sake of the higher interests themselves, that they do *not* receive exclusive attention. A broad and sane view of even the highest interest requires sympathetic understanding of many other interests. The reaction, too, in one's own case, which is certain to follow exclusive attention to any subject, is most disastrous to the interests which it was sought thus exclusively to conserve. Moreover, if one wishes to make some higher interest prevail with others, he must fulfil the conditions of influence, and these, again, we have seen, demand a broad range of interests. From every point of view, therefore, it is seen that no ideal interest can conquer by simple negation, and that no ideal interest has anything to gain by mere exclusiveness. For the denial of legitimate worldly interests only narrows the possible sphere of both morals and religion; it makes the ethical and the religious life less, not more, significant. For it is the glory of religion not to be set apart from life, but to permeate it powerfully.

So, too, in the supposed interests of religion, we too often lay exclusive emphasis on certain specific channels of revelation, and virtually deny that God is creator of any but a small part of his world, and thereby shut ourselves up against all other channels by which he might speak to us. This is no mean and narrow world in which we live, no cribbed and confined existence to which we are called. God made us complex, and there is no single avenue of approach to our being that he does not know, and through which he would not speak.

The history of philosophy corroborates the witness of psychology here with telling effect. Religion's most dangerous enemies have been nourished in its own fold, in this very spirit of exclusiveness. The mystics of the seventeenth century, for example, with their denial of the trustworthiness of the reason, which was made for the sake of exalting faith, definitely prepared the way for a sensationalism which ended logically in the French Enlightenment, with its attempt to sweep not only historic Christianity, but all religion and even morality from the earth.[1]

So, too, the weapon that in the years just past has been used most effectively against revealed religion — the doctrine of the relativity of human knowledge — was forged by Hamilton and Mansell in defense of Christianity. And to-day, no possible attacks upon Christianity from without are half so dangerous as the still too common assumption within of the actual and natural antagonism of faith and reason, of religion and science, of religion and morality, of the sacred and the secular. For the sake of exalting religion, we treat it as something utterly apart, only to pay the penalty of finding it, in the end, put utterly aside from the real life of man.

And the true significance, on the other hand, of some of the most hopeful religious movements of our time, is to be found in a genuine, even where half-unconscious, effort to bring religion everywhere into touch with life, and with *all* of life, to make man's relation to God a *reality*. This is the religious significance of such phenomena as the higher criticism, the greatly increasing reverence of men of science for religion, the growing

[1] *Cf.* Erdmann, *History of Philosophy*, Vol. II, pp. 99 ff.

insistence that all things are to be so used as to minister to the spirit,— that the whole world, according to Canon Fremantle's conception, is "the subject of redemption."

It follows that, just as exclusive attention to the higher interests has its inevitable reaction, so, too, the *absorption in the lower defeats itself*. A man's life can be no larger than the objects to which it is given. Things pass away, and even the desire for them fails. It is only he that does the will of God, St. John reminds us, and so gives himself to the really permanent, who abides forever. His life is poor indeed who has not gained a store of valuable and permanent interests. Without these, even the lower interests themselves must fail to give their full contribution. The full pulse of life cannot be felt without a wide range of interests, and a thoughtful relating of each to the rest of life.

We are learning to recognize, we may hope, the complexity of life.

It means much for rational living when the complexity of life has been fairly recognized with its logical consequences. For this implies that there can be no rule-of-thumb methods, no "patent process" character, no magical inheritance of results. In particular, this assertion of the complexity of life involves recognition of the paradoxes of life and emphasis on conditions. Both have direct suggestions for living, and may be made to include the most important, practical inferences from psychology's first great insistence — the complexity of life.

CHAPTER II

RECOGNITION OF THE PARADOXES OF LIFE—OPPOSING RELATIONS

ONE cannot face the problem set by the complicated relations of his existence without finding himself confronted again and again with the necessity of fulfilling relations seemingly opposed. Life constantly makes paradoxical demands upon us. And we have not admitted the complexity of life to much purpose if we have not seen, and in part, at least, solved the paradoxes that meet us in every sphere of our being.

I. THE ALL-INCLUSIVE PARADOX OF ENDS AND MEANS

Life itself is a paradox. Means seem often at war with ends, mechanism, with the ideals for which alone it exists. Only the ends are of absolute value, yet the means are indispensable to their attainment. The actual and necessary are not the ideal; the *is* and the *must* cannot give us the *ought*; and yet only through the use of the actual and necessary can anything ideal be achieved. And the question of the final harmony of mechanical means and ideal ends — the final harmony of the *is*, the *must*, and the *ought* — is for us all the question of questions. Its complete answer would be a final philosophy. So Lotze can make it the thesis of his entire philosophical system to " show how absolutely universal is the extent, and at the same time how completely subordinate the significance of the mission which mechanism has to fulfil in the structure of the world."[1]

II. THE PARADOXES OF THE DIFFERENT SPHERES OF LIFE

In the *physical* realm, as has been often noted, the paradox remains. The great hindrance to all motion is friction, yet without friction there can be no motion. There is an abiding animal body, yet every element of it is in flux. In our own physical life, there is a peculiar paradox; it is contained in the not infrequent phrase of our time — " power through repose." Physical

[1] *Microcosmus*, p. xvi.

relaxation *is* necessary to sustained energy; it is much to have learned really to relax strained muscles and nerves—to let go of oneself; yet relaxation may become nerveless, spineless flabbiness. We must learn to meet the paradox.

In the *intellectual* life no characteristic of consciousness is more marked than its selective nature, which contains in itself a paradox—the power to attend and the power to ignore; and the two most fundamental functions of intellectual activity are seemingly opposed—discrimination and assimilation—the discernment of likenesses and the discernment of differences. Sully suggests, after Aristotle, that the best mental habits are usually means between extremes, a combining of opposites. Thus a "skilful management of the memory" demands forgetting as well as remembering, "detecting what is important and overlooking what is unimportant." In the proper training of the imagination there must be both restraint and stimulation—restraint of immoderate fancy through developing judgment and reason, stimulus through furnishing materials and motive.[1]

[1] Sully, *Outlines of Psychology*, 1889, pp. 297, 326.

Our intellectual life is a constant struggle, too, between what Professor James calls "genius and old-fogyism"—between open-mindedness and conservatism, between perceiving the new as new and assimilating the new to the old; and neither factor can be given up. In James' words: "There is an everlasting struggle in every mind between the tendency to keep unchanged, and the tendency to renovate, its ideas. Our education is a ceaseless compromise between the conservative and the progressive factors." "Hardly any one of us can make new heads easily when fresh experiences come. Most of us grow more and more enslaved to the stock conceptions with which we have once become familiar, and less and less capable of assimilating impressions in any but the old ways. Old-fogyism, in short, is the inevitable terminus to which life sweeps us on." On the other hand, "genius, in truth, means little more than the faculty of perceiving in an unhabitual way."[1] An evident paradox confronts us here. We must seek to relate new knowledge to that already gained; but we must, at the same time, if there is to be any growth at all, be sure to recognize what is really

[1] *Psychology*, Vol. II, pp. 109, 110.

new, as new. So Sully says: "Excellence of judgment in this respect lies between two extremes of instability and obstinacy." "A sound judgment, too, combines a measure of intellectual independence with a due regard for the claims of others' convictions."[1]

The ideal is, while fully recognizing the new as new, to connect all new acquisitions *logically* with the old, making all needful readjustments to that end, and so to be able to command the whole store. This ideal is rarely fulfilled. It often happens that our ideas for a long time seem hardly to have met at all, and we wake up after some sudden bringing of them face to face, to find that we have been holding in our minds, with comfortable unconcern, ideas actually irreconcilable. Such a discovery may be epoch-making in a man's intellectual growth.

In *moral* life and influence, paradoxes repeatedly recur.

In *decision* a double demand is constantly laid upon us: make deliberation habitual, yet decide promptly when the evidence is once in. Great differences of temperament are to be recognized here; some children find it almost impossible to decide anything, while

[1] *Op. cit.*, p. 410.

others are uniformly precipitate in their decisions. Grizel, it will be remembered, said, "It is so easy to make up one's mind"; while "sentimental Tommy" replied, "It's easy to you that has just one mind, but if you had as many minds as I have——!" One needs to take these temperamental differences into account for himself and others; but the goal to be aimed at is clear. There must be neither the rash judgment that jumps at conclusions, nor the ever-hesitating judgment that finds decision almost impossible. There are circumstances in life when almost any prompt decision is of far more consequence than the best decision reached too late. "The ideal of a good character," another says, "is a combination of promptitude in following the right when the right is manifest, with wariness and a disposition to reflect and choose rationally and rightly whenever the right course is not at first apparent."[1]

Professor Palmer puts a similar paradox in his own way, when he says: "It is meaningless, then, to ask whether we should be intuitive and spontaneous, or considerate and deliberate. There is no such alternative.

[1] Sully, *Op. cit.*, p. 667.

We need both dispositions. We should seek to attain a condition of swift spontaneity, of abounding freedom, of the absence of all restraint, and should not rest satisfied with the conditions in which we were born. But we must not suffer that even the new nature should be allowed to become altogether natural. It should be but the natural engine for spiritual ends, itself repeatedly scrutinized with a view to their better fulfilment."[1] This view of the moral life is allied not only with the paradox in decision, but even more closely with the fundamental paradox of the moral life in self-assertion and self-surrender, considered a little later.

In the moral life, too, quietism wars with enthusiasm—the mood of the East with the mood of the West—and yet we can spare neither. To feel oneself in the grasp of a "vast and predestined order" stifles human initiative; but, on the other hand, to lose all sense of any plan larger than our own,—any on-working of universal forces, in line with which we may do our work, is to take the heart out of our work, and to make a *life-calling* impossible. A true quietism is, thus, the very root of a genuine enthusiasm.

[1] *The Nature of Goodness*, p. 240.

We must be able to reach Browning's "All's love, yet all's law."

In this very conviction of the complexity of life which we have been considering, there is a particularly difficult paradox to be faced. With this broad conviction of the essential complexity of life, how are we to combine a *true simplicity?* What is the real demand of the simple life? Does it mean cutting off or ignoring any sides of our being? We have already seen that ideal interests cannot gain by a spirit of exclusiveness. But the true breadth is not lack of discrimination. It is but a poor and illogical protest against the Puritan's indiscriminate condemnation of much that was good, to react to an equally indiscriminate acceptance either of good and bad alike, or of all goods as of equal value. A self-indulgent and merely sporting people cannot be a great people. But a true simplicity and a reasonable recognition of the complexity of life alike call for a discrimination that can both recognize all goods as goods, and yet see and rigorously treat the lesser goods as lesser; and that means, if need be, the sacrifice of the lesser unhesitatingly to the greater. This is both the broad and the simple life.

So, too, there is the further paradox of emotion to be shunned, and emotion to be welcomed. The false emotion that exhausts, — the strain that is drain, the forced, the high-strung, the hysterical, — is at perpetual war with the true emotion that invigorates, that comes, that is not manufactured, and that is the sign of reserved power. And one of the great weaknesses, as we shall see, both in friendship and in religion, is failure to discriminate clearly these two kinds of emotions.

Even in *influence* there is a paradox, and the solution is not so easy as is often assumed; for there are two kinds of "weaker brethren"; — not only those for whom eating flesh is sin and whom you stumble by eating, but also those for whom it is no sin, and whom you stumble by making it a sin. Between these two classes one has always to guide his course; both are to be regarded; both lay duties upon us. And the duty of developing a proper conscience in another may often be as imperative as the duty of removing all possible temptation from his path. It is often very difficult to decide which duty is paramount in a given case. One needs, at the very least, to be sure that his decision is not determined by his own selfish desire.

Religion, too, has to steer between a superstitiousness that sees the magically supernatural everywhere, and a materialistic realism that sees God nowhere. It must have a firm hold on ideals, on the spiritual world, or lose its very existence; but it must believe as well that these ideals can be realized through mechanical means, or give up any power in actual life. The religious man must be "humbly-proud," as Erdmann says,—humble in view of the eternal and infinite plans of God; proud, as called to a possible and an "imperishable work in the world."

In similar fashion, religion has to find its way between rationalism and mysticism. It can have no war with reason; but it must insist that the true reason must take account of all the data—emotional and volitional as well as intellectual—that a man can feel and do and experience more than he can tell. It must deny, therefore, both a narrow intellectualism and an irrational mysticism. To keep the two tendencies in proper balance is one of the pressing problems of a man's personal religious life.

The *choosing of one's lifework and one's abiding character*, again, is a choice among several possible *mes*, which, however good separately, cannot possibly coexist. "Not that I would not, if I could," says James, "be both handsome and fat and well-dressed, and a great athlete, and make a million a year, be a wit, a *bon-vivant*, and a lady-killer as well as a philosopher; a philanthropist, statesman, warrior, and African explorer, as well as a 'tone-poet' and saint. But the thing is simply impossible. The millionaire's work would run counter to the saint's; the *bon-vivant* and the philanthropist would trip each other up; the philosopher and the lady-killer could not well keep house in the same tenement of clay. . . . So the seeker of his truest, strongest, deepest self must review the list carefully and pick out the one on which he is to stake his salvation."[1]

But this one "me" being chosen, even then the future potential better self is always at war with the present, however good. One can build only on the present self, yet he must leave it behind. He must both deny it and affirm it. The ideal potential self passes continual judgment on the present self.

The problem of life becomes, thus, everywhere a paradox, which can be definitely stated. A fundamental paradox is

[1] *Psychology*, Vol. I, pp. 309, 310.

involved in our very natures, as is perhaps indicated most clearly by Professor Royce's classification of mental phenomena[1]. He denotes two of the three fundamental heads of his classification as *docility* and *initiative*, and defines these terms as follows: "By the docility of an animal we mean the capacity shown in its acts to adjust these acts not merely to a present situation, but to the relation between this present situation and what has occurred in the former life of this organism. . . . The term 'docility' is chosen as a convenient name *both* for the physical manifestation of the animal's power to profit by experience, and for the mental processes that accompany this same power." In this sense, docility gives us the law of habit. "Its interpretation in terms of consciousness is, that any conscious process which is of a type that has occurred before tends to recur more readily, up to the point where the limit of training has been reached, and to displace rival conscious processes, according as its type has frequently occurred." And the law of habit involves the law of association, "the assimilation of new habits to old ones," and, in the social life, the constant influence of imitation.

[1] *Outlines of Psychology*, pp. viii, x, 38, 53, 198, 234, 279, etc.

On the other hand, "The sort of mental initiative which is especially in question in the present discussion is that which appears when already acquired, and intelligent habits are decidedly altered, or are decidedly recombined, in such fashion as to bring to pass a novel readjustment to our environment." This is the recognition of "critical points" in our development. Now, our mental life and growth manifestly require both docility and initiative; each must have its due place and recognition. And this fundamental paradox involves many lesser ones. It appears, as has been already seen, in the intellectual life; it appears also in character, and in any large and wise management of life.

Character, in the large sense, requires both self-assertion and self-surrender, both individuality and deference, both the assertion of a law for oneself and the reasonable yielding to others, both loyalty to conviction and open-mindedness, both free independence and obedience. "In brief," says Royce, "the preservation of a happy balance between the imitative functions and those that emphasize social contrasts and oppositions forms the basis for every higher type of mental activity. And the entire process of conscious education involves the deliberate appeal to the docility of these two types of social instincts.[1] For, whatever else we teach to a social being, we teach him to imitate; and whatever use we teach him to make of his social imitations in his relations with other men, we are obliged at the same time to teach him to assert himself, in some sort of way, in contrast with his fellows, and by virtue of the arts which he possesses."

No wonder the child is often honestly perplexed, and not a little dazed, at times, to find himself blamed for disobedience, where he felt himself really standing for principle. Yet it is certain that without a good large admixture of self-assertion to give him backbone, the child will be mere clay under the influence of his surroundings and can never form character.[2]

No wonder the grown man, too, frequently mistakes. Lecky gives a particular illustration of this paradox in character, in speaking of

[1] I cannot help thinking that it would have been more logical for Professor Royce to have regarded these two contrasted instincts as illustrations respectively of his two fundamental contrasts of "docility" and "initiative"; and I have here so treated them. After the great emphasis of his fundamental classification of mental phenomena, his actual treatment of "initiative" seems needlessly disappointing.

[2] *Cf.* King, *The Appeal of the Child*, p. 48.

the difficulties of "parliamentary government worked upon party lines." "It needs," he says, "a combination of independence and discipline which is not common, and where it does not exist parliaments speedily degenerate either into an assemblage of puppets in the hands of party leaders or into disintegrated, demoralized, insubordinate groups."[1] The same paradoxical combination of qualities is indicated again by Lecky as necessary, when he says: "One of the worst moral evils that grow up in democratic countries is the excessive tendency to time-serving and popularity-hunting, and the danger is all the greater because in a certain sense both of these things are a necessity and even a duty. Their moral quality depends mainly on their motive."[2] This problem is thus a perpetual one. The solution cannot be easy for child or parent, for student or teacher, for citizen or government. Kindly, patient suggestion, which is reverent of the individual person, earnest seeking of the best that is attainable in the circumstances, and honest coöperation are needed.

So, too, a similar paradox confronts us in

[1] *The Map of Life*, p. 183.
[2] *Op. cit.*, p. 141.

the general conduct of our lives. In Lecky's words, "To maintain in their due proportion in our nature the spirit of content and the desire to improve, to combine a realized appreciation of the blessings we enjoy with a healthy and well-regulated ambition, is no easy thing, but it is the problem which all who aspire to a perfect life should set before themselves."[1]

The final solution of this fundamental paradox of self-surrender and self-assertion for a finite being would apparently be reached only when one had found a self-surrender, which included all lesser surrenders, and was, at the same time, the completest self-assertion — a yielding which should be, also, the boldest "claim on life." Such a solution, Christ evidently believes that he finds in his recurring paradox of saving the life by losing it — denying the narrow, merely individual self, like the grain of wheat in the ground, to rise to the life of the larger self. Every surrender to a high friendship is, as Ritschl has pointed out, "not a weakening denial of self, but a strengthening affirmation of self," for love itself is life, the largest life. But in the supreme surrender to the will of God,

[1] *Op. cit.*, p. 28.

we welcome and share the supreme and all-sufficing life; and here, as Professor Everett contended against Nietsche's position, one finds in truth his own highest and strongest self-assertion. "Religion," in Biedermann's language, "is the lifting of life out of dependence on its circumstances into the freedom which comes from absolute dependence."

But a paradox is not solved by stating it, or even by indicating the ideal combination. There must be a tracing out of the actual relations involved, a discerning of the multiplied conditions upon which the solution depends. Psychology can be a science only so far as it is actually able to discover these conditions. And the emphasis of psychology on the complexity and paradox of life means, therefore, at the same time, emphasis on conditions.

CHAPTER III

THE EMPHASIS OF PSYCHOLOGY ON CONDITIONS

THE insistence of psychology on the complexity and paradox of life means emphasis on conditions; for if all life is so inter-related, and so puzzlingly complex, we can make progress in the knowledge and in the living of it, only in so far as we regard these actual relations and fulfil these matter-of-fact conditions. Something like this is attempted by Lecky in his very suggestive book, *The Map of Life*, already quoted. Perhaps the most striking thing in the book is its insistence upon what the author calls "the importance of compromise in practical life." This might, perhaps, better be called the intelligent, practical, and detailed recognition of the *complexity* of life; for no real compromise of principle is anywhere involved. But Lecky's main thought is certainly justified, and is an immediate inference from the conviction of the complexity of life, as is indicated by his own statement: "Life is a scene in which different kinds of interest not only blend but also modify and in some degree counterbalance one another, and it can only be carried on by constant compromises in which the lines of definition are seldom very clearly marked, and in which even the highest interest must not altogether absorb or override the others."[1] And he discusses with great care and insight the necessity of such "compromise" in war, in the law, in politics, and in the Church.

Certainly the problem of the practical solution of the complexity of life through recognition of the precise relations and conditions involved cannot be escaped by any man who wishes to live a wise and righteous life. There must be both the knowledge and the fulfilment of precise conditions.

I. THE LESSONS OF NATURAL SCIENCE

This is the lesson of the marvelous growth of the natural sciences: unwearied study of minute details; patient search for the law underlying the phenomena investigated, and for the exact conditions involved; precise and persistent fulfilment of these condi-

[1] *Op. cit.*, pp. 90, 91.

tions. So science grows, and so its problems are solved. It discerns law, and hence possible achievement. That is, we accomplish nothing except through the forces of nature. We can use these only so far as we see their laws and fulfil the conditions required; and this fulfilment requires time. Law, conditions, time! So and so only has man's dominion over nature come about; so and so only can dominion over one's own nature be achieved, and life's problem solved.

Because the problem of life is complex, we must attack it as the scientist attacks his problem, with a definite conviction of law and with consequent hope. Drummond's greatest contribution to his generation lay in this insistence upon law in the moral and spiritual world. This conviction withdraws the moral and spiritual from the realm of the magical and brings in hope of real achievement. So believing, we may set the laws of the world and of the mind working for us, and have patience with ourselves and with others. There are laws in the spiritual world; we can find them out; we can know their implied conditions; these conditions we can fulfil; and we can so count confidently upon results. Otherwise, the perception of the complexity of life could bring only baffling confusion. There must be definite conditions of growth, of character, of happiness, of influence. And it is psychology's highest task to instruct us as to these conditions of our own life.

II. THE SIGNIFICANCE OF COMMON WORK AND DUTIES

And just here lie, too, for practical living, the seriousness and value of common every-day work and of prosaic duties, as the clearest-sighted have always seen. It is in these that the actual essential conditions come out most clearly. It is interesting to notice that the very language of our most wise and useful proverbs shows that they have been wrought out in the realm of common toil of various kinds. We shall certainly not solve our greater and more distant problems by ignoring those smaller and more immediate. Because of the complex intertwining of things, as in science, so in life, we can never safely slight small matters. Our principles never so plainly rule as when they lead us to care in their slighter, more delicate, and more thoughtful manifestations.

It is true that in sight of the infinite goal, the exercises and aims and discords of our daily living may seem petty enough,—"and yet," as Lotze says—and I know no nobler passage in all his writing—"and yet we must continue these exercises, devote to these contracted aims all the ardor of our souls, painfully feel these discords, and again and again renew the conflict concerning them; our life would not be ennobled by depreciation of its conditions, and of the stage which it offers to our struggling energy." We get control of the principles of life only by some real working of them out,—only by the laboratory method.

Here lies the significance of Lowell's "work done squarely and unwasted days"; of Gannett's new beatitude, "Blessed be drudgery"; of the Bishop of Exeter's statement, that "of all work that produces results, nine-tenths must be drudgery." And there is to be, too, no "blue-rose melancholy," that thinks it could do great things if conditions were altogether otherwise—if the roses were only blue. We are called to face the exact circumstances in which we are, and faithfully to fulfil the conditions there demanded.

III. NO MAGICAL INHERITANCE

In the best things, then, there can be no short-cuts, no sudden leaps, no transcendental flights, no magical inheritance in vision. Long periods of gradual growth precede the harvest. Steady fulfilment of conditions—daily, hourly, detailed, faithful—can alone bring great hours of vision, and can alone make great hours of vision fruitful. The vision of the goal is inspiring, but it must not make us discontented with the road thereto. Dreaming of the goal is not attainment of it, nor is working oneself up to belief in a goal already attained. It is far safer for us to say with one of the world's best fighters, "I count not myself yet to have apprehended," than to sing with the modern religionist, "I've reached the land of corn and wine."

Character and acquaintance—the two best things in the gift of life, and the very essence of religion—are both growths and active achievements, never a magical inheritance. They are not given outright, and God himself cannot so create them. They can only *become* in time and under conditions; but this time given and these conditions fulfilled, you can count on results. This is the point of that remarkable modern stanza of E. R. Sill:

> " Forenoon, and afternoon, and night;— Forenoon,
> And afternoon, and night; Forenoon, and — what?
> The empty song repeats itself. No more?
> Yea, that is life; make this forenoon sublime,
> This afternoon a psalm, this night a prayer,
> And time is conquered, and thy crown is won."

IV. NO CONDITIONS IN GENERAL

But — and we need to heed it — there are no conditions in general, only conditions in particular. We develop power or character not by a general striving, not by resolving in general, but only by definite, concrete applications in definite relations. This ignoring of the particular is one of the great errors, both of common asceticism and of common mysticism. General self-denial and general surrender to God that involve no particulars in actual life are fruitless enough. On the contrary, general forms or types of activity, "a given 'set' of the brain as a whole," may result from repeated particular associated acts. So Royce says: "It is known, for instance, that 'fickleness' of conduct, irrational change of plan of behavior, can itself become a hopelessly fixed habit in a given brain."[1]

There is the more need of insistence upon the careful pointing out of the precise particular conditions in the moral and spiritual life, both because of the marked scientific temper of our times, and because the natural temperament of the reformer or the religious worker, with its emphasis upon ideals, is often accompanied by theoretical vagueness and an unwillingness to use practical means, and so tends to make him neglectful of accurate study of the precise conditions for the attainment of these ideals. It is a great thing for a man to combine vision of the ideal with the scientific method; this calls for the best in two opposing temperaments — the sentimental and the choleric.

What answer, now, has psychology to make to the inquiry for the exact conditions on which growth depends? Our second great inference from psychology should suggest the actual conditions — bodily and mental; for modern psychology emphasizes the unity of man — the unity of mind and body, and the unity of the mind itself.

[1] *Outlines of Psychology*, p. 69; *cf.* also James' *Psychology*, Vol. I, p. 126.

THE UNITY OF MAN

CHAPTER IV

THE UNITY OF MIND AND BODY—INTRODUCTION

It is the unity of mind and body which it has been the special mission of physiological psychology to bring out. And the assertion of such unity certainly means, to begin with, that, for the present world at least, the intellectual and moral and spiritual life has its bodily conditions. This is to be said neither boastingly nor cynically. It is to be faced as a simple fact. We have bodies, and we cannot set ourselves free from them.

I. ASCETIC TREATMENT OF BODILY CONDITIONS

The long sad history of asceticism in all lands shows how real the religious life has felt this connection with the body to be, and at the same time how fiercely it has resented it. Men have remained, in this question of asceticism, quite too largely on the mythological plane, without any clear sense of a real nature and unity of things. The scientific spirit, which demands a careful study of detailed connections and conditions, has had little enough to do with this blind, fierce struggle; and, in consequence, the ascetic has everywhere, on the one hand, failed to take any sensible account of the effects of ordinary bodily conditions; and, on the other hand, paradoxically enough, has exalted the effects of certain abnormal bodily conditions into higher spiritual attainments.[1] These historical results of religious asceticism certainly cannot be held to commend the method of ignoring bodily conditions. The plain lesson of modern science here would seem to be, that, if the spirit is ever to master the body, it must know its laws and take account of its conditions; these are the very instruments of its mastery. So, and only so, has science made nature serve it.

One can quite understand the reluctance of the spiritual life to admit the closeness of its connection with the physical. It seems itself to be lowered thereby. But it gets no freedom and power by vehemently denying the fact, and ignoring the resulting conditions. Rather, its superiority must be shown, its freedom and power declared, as has been

[1] *Cf.* Royce, *Op. cit.*, pp. 125, 126.

implied, by patient study of the laws of this body and of its connection with the spirit, and by steady fulfilment of the conditions by which alone mastery can come. It is a false and abstract spiritualism, therefore, that hesitates clearly to recognize or to affirm the bodily conditions of the spiritual life. Let us frankly admit that much of the dissatisfaction of the moral and spiritual life results from a wholly unnecessary and senseless disregard of bodily conditions. The emphasis of modern psychology upon the close connection of body and mind, thus, compels the thoughtful man to a study of the bodily conditions of true living.

II. NOT A MATERIALISTIC POSITION

But, from the religious point of view, it is exactly this emphasis of modern psychology and of allied views in biology which seems to many to make impossible any independent or enduring life of the spirit at all. A genuinely religious view of the world seems to them precluded by the known facts of biology and of physiological psychology. The difficulty is a very real one to-day, in the case of hundreds of students and of many others.

If, therefore, we leave aside for the present the deeper question of a final idealistic view of the world, we shall still need to show that this bodily connection and its implied conditions involve no denial of the spiritual life itself.

The precise difficulty felt is this: the affirmation of bodily conditions for the spiritual life seems to many, even of those uninfluenced by modern psychological views, virtually to assert that the material facts are primary, the spiritual secondary; that the body is the real independent variable, and that psychical states are in truth but results of bodily or brain states, and hence, that at least no continued life of the spirit could be affirmed after the destruction of the brain.

In answer to the difficulty, one might content himself with simply calling attention to the fact that so distinguished a psychologist, for example, as Professor James, with all that modern biology and psychology have to say distinctly in mind, expressly asserts that not only is there no scientific reason for denying the independent reality of the spirit now, but there is also none for denying the possibility of its continued existence after the body. The spiritual life is certainly not precluded, then, by modern psychology[1]. And it is a misconception of its teachings that asserts this.

But the difficulty is for many so serious, that it is probably worth while to see for ourselves just where the misconception lies. And, fortunately, some present general admissions of scientists make the way here much shorter, even from a dualistic point of view, than it could have been some years ago. It is a most noteworthy fact that materialism as a philosophical theory has practically vanished even from the ranks of natural scientists; that modern science expressly denies that it is materialistic. It has been driven to take this position, not because it could not show *how* brain states could pass into psychical states, for it cannot be said to understand the final *how* anywhere; but because, to affirm that brain states were the true causes of psychical states, would deny its fundamental doctrine of the conservation of energy[2]. It would be to affirm that what was simply a mode of motion in the brain disappeared as such altogether, and reappeared as something not at all a mode of

[1] See James, *Human Immortality*, pp. 7–30.
[2] See Paulsen, *Introduction to Philosophy*, pp. 74 ff.

motion. This would involve an absolute break in the physical series, an annihilation of motion, and a virtual creation of something else. A completer denial of the conservation of energy could not be made. The natural scientist, therefore, has quite abandoned, on grounds that for him are imperative, the old position that the brain states are the *cause* of psychical states.

From the present standpoint of the natural scientist, therefore, we may not only say with Professor James,[1] that we have no need to assert a "*productive* function" of the brain in its relation to the psychical states, since we may equally well assume a "permissive" or "transmissive function"; but we may say, we cannot admit the possibility of a *productive* function of the brain, since it would deny the conservation of energy. To the strict logic of the position involved in the doctrine of the conservation of energy, naturalism must be held. That position only allows it to recognize two continuous mutually independent series — the one physical, the other psychical — equally justified as facts. And this necessary admission is quite sufficient for our present purpose, which was

[1] *Human Immortality*, p. 15.

simply to show that physiological psychology does not preclude the conviction of a real and independent spiritual life.

That there are many reasons for questioning the absolute dualism of this conception of the relation of the physical and the psychical; that naturalism is itself most inconsistent in carrying out its position, since, as Ward points out, "though rejecting materialism" it "abandons neither the materialistic standpoint nor the materialistic endeavor to colligate the facts of life, mind and history with a mechanical scheme";[1] that the whole philosophy underlying it is hardly capable of any final defense;—all this need not now concern us. It is enough for the present that we are at liberty to speak in ordinary terms of the bodily conditions of the spiritual life, without any logically implied denial of the independent reality and significance of that spiritual life.

Returning, then, from this long digression, let us notice that these modern investigations do not allow us to forget that man—mind and body—is a real unity, two-sided and complex enough it may be, yet one and not two; they leave us no room to doubt the

[1] *Naturalism and Agnosticism*, Vol. I, p. viii.

mysterious intimacy of the connection of the physical and the psychical. It is more than alliteration when Höffding[1] insists on "the parallelism and proportionality," and Sully[2] insists on "the concomitance and covariation" of the nervous and mental processes.

[1] *Outlines of Psychology*, pp. 50 ff.
[2] *Op. cit.*, p. 4.

CHAPTER V

THE UNITY OF MIND AND BODY—THE PSYCHOLOGICAL EVIDENCE

I. THE LAW OF DIFFUSION

ONE of the clearest proofs of this intimate connection of the psychical with the physical —not in the case of the brain only, but in the whole body—is contained in what Bain has called the law of diffusion, and which James thus states: "Using sweeping terms, and ignoring exceptions, we might say that every possible feeling produces a movement, and that movement is a movement of the entire organism, and of each and all its parts. What happens patently when an explosion or a flash of lightning startles us, or when we are tickled, happens latently with every sensation we receive."[1] These effects of feeling, even of the simplest kind, on the body, have been experimentally traced in the modification of the circulation of the blood, of respiration, of the activity of the sweat

[1] *Op. cit.*, Vol. II, p. 372.

glands, and of the voluntary muscles, and less accurately in movements of the viscera. To take but a single instance, the effect on circulation: every least mental activity — feeling or thought — affects the circulation of the blood. This is particularly striking in the brain.

Mosso's ingenious experiments here [1] make the connection of thought and circulation of blood in the brain incontestable. He placed his subjects upon a table so carefully balanced that the slightest increase of weight at either extremity would turn the scale. He found that any active thinking by the subject, like the solving of a problem, would at once cause the head end of the table to go down, in consequence of the influx of blood to the head. Sometimes the subject went to sleep on this "scientific cradle," and it was found that even in sleep so slight a disturbance as the moving of a chair was enough to cause brain activity sufficient to call for such influx of blood as to make the head end of the table go down.

Henle has shown, also, that the depressing emotions increase the contraction of the

[1] *Cf.*, e. g., James, *Op. cit.*, Vol. I, p. 98; *Pedagogical Seminary*, Vol. II, p. 12.

smooth unstriped muscles of the arteries, skin, and bronchial tubes, while exciting emotions make them relax, and so believes himself able to trace even the "natural history of the sigh."[1]

II. PSYCHICAL EFFECTS OF BODILY TRAINING

The influence of *bodily training* on mind and morals is another indication of the close relation of body and mind. The localization of the centers of motion in the brain make it natural to expect that all definitely directed movements will directly affect the brain, and so mental development. Du Bois Reymond[2] says explicitly that "it is easy to demonstrate that such bodily exercises as gymnastics, fencing, swimming, riding, dancing and skating are much more exercises of the central nervous system, of the brain and spinal marrow" than of the muscles. These theoretical anticipations are abundantly confirmed by the facts. The success of the experiments of Dr. Sequin in the training of idiots, beginning with a year's training devoted mainly to the hand, is one such fact.

[1] James, *Psychology*, Vol. II, p. 445.
[2] *Popular Science Monthly*, Vol. XXI, p. 325.

Such results as those attained in the physical training department of the New York State Reformatory, at Elmira, furnish further evidence in the same direction. The careful records kept of the men in this prison, in shop work, in school work, and in conduct, make these experiments peculiarly valuable; and these records show incontestable mental and moral gain from physical training.[1] The Director testified, after several years of direct experiment and observation, that "physical education inculcates habits of obedience, mental concentration, and application, and forces into the background the former man."

III. THE CLOSE CONNECTION OF THE WILL AND MUSCULAR ACTIVITY

The ethical life with its center in the will is particularly interested in the close connection between muscular activity and the will, which modern psychology is asserting.

Sully puts the principle clearly and briefly: "On the one side," he says, "attention involves a certain amount of motor innervation and muscular activity. On the other side,

[1] *Cf.* entire article, *Muscle and Mind*, F. E. White, *Popular Science Monthly*, Vol. XXXV, pp. 377 ff.

all voluntary movement involves attention." "All practice in doing things, then, whatever its primary object may be, is, to some extent, a strengthening of volitional power." So Stanley Hall urges: "Few realize . . . how impossible healthful energy of will is without strong muscles which are its organ, or how endurance and self-control, no less than great achievement, depend on muscle-habits."[1] In confirmation of this principle, it is particularly worth noting that in Dr. Maclaren's inquiry of the men of the Cambridge and Oxford University crews of many years, it was found that the benefits from their training, which the men made most of, were "increase of stamina, of energy, enterprise, and executive power, and of fortitude in endurance of trials, privations, and disappointments"— all distinctly volitional gains.

Most men of much less specialized physical training, who have given the matter thought, can similarly bear witness to an influx of volitional energy from reasonable muscular activity. Definite bodily exercise seems often as distinctly volitional as physical in its effects. There is a close connection between muscular tone and will-power, which the man who

[1] *Pedagogical Seminary*, Vol. II, p. 75.

seeks complete self-control will do well to heed. James carries the suggestion a step further, when he says: "And that blessed internal peace and confidence, that *acquiescentia in se ipso*, as Spinoza used to call it, that wells up from every part of the body of a muscularly well-trained human being, and soaks the indwelling soul of him with satisfaction, is, quite apart from every consideration of its mechanical utility, an element of spiritual hygiene of supreme significance."[1]

We have no right to ignore the bodily conditions of a rational life here implied. The greatly increased interest on all sides in bodily exercise has a plain and genuine contribution to make, even to the spiritual life. And the passing of some morbid religious questionings, too, has in this fact, I suspect, a practical explanation. I have, myself, a good deal of faith in the value of the coming muscular minister.

The increasingly certain outcome of the concentrated observation and experiment of the last thirty years, by physiological psychology in this field, confirmed by most varied practical application, is that all real training is training, whether it be of the whole body,

[1] *Talks on Psychology and Life's Ideals*, p. 207.

manual, industrial, purely mental, or moral; that man is so far one that real training anywhere helps training everywhere, and consequently, also, that neglect anywhere means something of loss everywhere.

IV. THE PHYSICAL BASIS OF HABIT

But nowhere are the psychical and physical so completely interwoven as in the phenomena of habit. The mind's initiative constantly comes in, but it is as constantly seconded by the nervous system. The physiological basis of habit consists in the plasticity of the nerve substance, and in the capacity of nerve substance to receive and retain impressions. There results the certainty that the nervous system will act again more easily in those ways in which it has already acted. The nervous system behaves here with dreadful impartiality.

Habits man must have, but it is for him to choose what they shall be, provided he chooses quickly. The *time-limit in habits* is one of the strong evidences of the close connection of body and mind. It is a startling fact to face, that a man's personal habits are largely fixed before he is twenty; the chief lines of his future growth and acquaintance before he is twenty-five, and his professional habits before he is thirty; yet to something like this, James believes, physiological psychology points.[1] Our intellectual as well as our moral day of grace is limited. It is of no use to rebel at the facts, it is folly unspeakable to ignore them. We are becoming bundles of habits. With every young person one must, therefore, continually urge: Are you willing to retain just the *personal* habits you have now? You cannot too quickly change them if you wish to make thorough work. From your early morning toilet, through the care of your clothing and the order of your room, table manners, breathing, tone of voice, manner of talking, pronunciation, gesture, motion, address, study, to your very way of sleeping at night — all your habits are setting like plaster of Paris. Do you wish them to set as they are?

But this insistence upon a general time-limit in habits must not be pressed unduly. As Royce says, "the cortex remains, to a remarkably late period in life, persistently sensitive to a great variety of new impressions, and capable of forming at least a certain

[1] *Op. cit.*, pp. 121, 122.

number of specialized new habits — such as are involved whenever we learn to recognize and name a new acquaintance, or to carry out a new business enterprise."[1]

V. THE EVIDENCE OF HYPNOTISM

The facts concerning hypnotism may be taken as a final evidence of the exceeding closeness of the relation of mind and body. The marked effect of the hypnotic sleep upon memory, and the well-nigh incredible susceptibility to suggestion which it produces, are among the facts which show, as Baldwin says, "an intimacy of interaction between mind and body, to which current psychology in its psycho-physical theories is only beginning to do justice."[2]

[1] *Outlines of Psychology*, p. 66.
[2] *Mental Development, Methods and Processes*, p. 165.

CHAPTER VI

THE UNITY OF MIND AND BODY — SUGGESTIONS FOR LIVING

WHAT suggestions, now, has this unity of man — mind and body — for wise living? This mysterious unity of man is a reminder that no conditions are really trivial, that no member of this unity can suffer alone, and that character has bodily conditions as well as psychical, that may not be ignored. These physical conditions, it may be repeated, are only conditions, not causes; but they *are* conditions.

I. THE BODY INFLUENCES THE MIND

There is no help for it. However it may be in the future, one is not yet a disembodied spirit. One must face present conditions. What does this mean?

The Need of Well-oxygenated Blood. — It means, for one thing, that one must plan for blood, good blood, enough blood, and well-oxygenated blood. And this not simply for physical comfort, but for the sake of rational thinking and righteous living. The facts already given as to the law of diffusion should prove this. One of the first authorities in the country on nervous diseases asserts that many forms of insanity are not due to organic lesions of the brain, but are probably to be attributed to a "functional change in the brain due to disordered nutrition or circulation."[1] Corning's experiments in artificially hindering the flow of blood to the head tend to the same conclusion.[2]

Still later investigations of Mosso on the phenomena of fatigue,[3] as well as those of LaGrange on the physiology of bodily exercise, emphasize the fact that the *quality* of the blood is an equally necessary condition of normal brain activity. "The substances produced by overworking the brain and all other organs," Mosso says in effect, "are drosses," the great part of which ought to be burned up by aid of the oxygen of the blood. "Fatigue, thus, bodily and mental, is a sort of poisoning by the

[1] Starr, *Diseases of the Mind*, p. 27.
[2] *Cf.* Corning, *Brain Exhaustion*, pp. 37 ff.
[3] See *Pedagogical Seminary*, Vol. II, pp. 267, 268.

chemical products of decomposition." LaGrange,[1] lays emphasis on the fact that the great gain of exercise is that a man "lays up a provision of oxygen" and so produces what he calls "more living blood." And the feeling of drowsiness — brain-workers should note — often means need of oxygen rather than need of sleep.

This is no matter of mere bodily hygiene; it is quite certain to become a question of morals. The influence of brain-congestion or anæmia (and only in less degree of the supply of vitiated blood to the brain) upon the temper and disposition is immediate and marked. The language of specialists upon this point is so strong that it would seem to you extravagant if I should quote it. Thus Hammond speaks of the "whole character changed by a slight attack of cerebral congestion."

This means, then, that a man has no business to be too lazy to breathe, and breathe deeply, or to exercise sufficiently, or to fulfil any of the conditions for enough good oxygenated living blood. One may well be reminded that the authorities agree that feeling is no safe test as to the amount of exercise needed. It should not be for-

[1] *The Physiology of Bodily Exercise.*

gotten, on the other hand, as Corning suggests,[1] that there may be excessive development and use of the muscular system, especially in people with limited digestive power; but the temptation of brain-workers is, doubtless, not generally in that direction. Because of the "close analogy between the effects of mental fatigue and those of muscular fatigue," LaGrange speaks of "the dangers of mere physical exercise without diminution of brain work," and expressly recommends simple exercises as best for brain-workers.[2] Temptations enough we are certain to meet; we have no right needlessly to increase them. Yet blood is not the first and chief factor in attention, Mosso says, but nerve power.

The Need of Surplus Nervous Energy. Effects of Fatigue.[3]—Particularly important, therefore, in the bearing on both intellectual and moral efficiency, are *the facts as to fatigue*.

The Effect of Fatigue on Attention and

---

[1] *Brain Exhaustion*, pp. 47, 188 ff.
[2] *Op cit.*, pp. 351; 339 ff., 379 ff.
[3] *Cf.* on the whole, Burnham, *School Hygiene;* Dresslar, *Fatigue;* and Chamberlain on Mosso, *Pedagogical Seminary*, Vol. II, pp. 9 ff., 102 ff., 267 ff.; and, for many illustrations, Coe, *The Spiritual Life*, pp. 71 ff.

Self-Control.—The facts as to fatigue are important, for one reason, because scientific observation seems to show that *natural* power of self-control is directly proportioned to the amount of surplus nervous energy. "The phenomena of inhibition are the stronger," says Höffding, "the fuller the organism is of life, and weaker when the organism is in a state of fatigue." "In this respect the condition of the central organ is of decisive influence."[1] All self-control seems to involve the use of the higher brain centers which are first affected by fatigue or any abuse, and self-control becomes increasingly difficult as these centers are overtasked. Brain-fag, Beard says, brings inability to bear responsibility, defective and uncertain will, lack of power to inhibit, while "perfect inhibition is the sign of perfect health."

But power of self-control lies at the foundation of all intellectual attainment and of any possible character. Control of appetites and passions, even the lowest degree of prudence, to say nothing of unselfish subordination of one's own interests, rests directly upon the power of self-control. There can be no growth in practical wisdom, or progress

[1] *Op. cit.*, p. 44.

toward a better self—mental or moral—for one who cannot hold the present in abeyance to the future. The cardinal difference between the sane and the insane, even, lies in self-control. Dr. Starr says, "its deficiency is universally regarded as evidence of mental instability." It is, therefore, of no small moral interest to determine the bodily conditions of self-control.

In a general way, every one knows from experience that when he is tired it is harder to be decent. But the more recent investigations of physiological psychologists into the phenomena of fatigue give needed emphasis and point to this observation. Psychologically, the power of self-control consists chiefly in the power of attention, the power to hold steadily before one the future advantage, the reasons for the better course, the broader wisdom, in spite of the incitements of present impulse. Now, the most careful observations yet made,—those of Mosso,—show that "attention is the chief condition of mental fatigue," and this means that fatigue directly hinders the power of attention and consequently the power of self-control. That is, we are dealing here with the immediate physical conditions of will-power. What, then, are the facts about fatigue, what are its conditions and signs?

Direct Effect of Fatigue on Nerve Conditions.—The importance of surplus nervous energy is emphasized by all specialists in this field. Dr. Clouston says, "Exhaustion of nervous energy always lessens the inhibitory power" and speaks of "reserve brain-power—that most valuable of all brain qualities." Dr. J. M. Granville says: "The part which 'a stock of energy' plays in brain work can scarcely be exaggerated."[1] Dr. W. H. Burnham, after reviewing all the recent important investigations of this kind in the world, emphasizes the fact that in the nervous system "only a limited amount of energy is available at any moment"; and "the one essential thing in economic brain action is the maintenance of the proper balance between the storage and expenditure of energy." Fatigue is the sign that the reserve stock is being drawn upon, that one has begun to consume his principal. To continue work in spite of warnings of weariness is simply to drug the watchman of the treasury. Direct experiment in electrical stimulation of the nerve-cells of frogs and cats shows a "remark-

[1] *Popular Science Monthly*, Vol. XX, p. 104.

able shrinking of the nerve-cells, particularly of the nuclei." After five hours' continuous work, the cell nucleus is only half its normal size, and twenty-four hours of rest are necessary for complete restoration to its normal state. But half the amount of work, it is particularly worth noting, does not require nearly half the amount of time for recovery. In experiments by Dr. Hodge on nerve-cells of animals, Burnham says that a remarkable difference was found between the condition of the cells in the morning and at night; "for example, in the brain-cells of honey-bees taken at night the nuclei had shrunken about a third." "Of course," he adds, "we cannot apply just the same figures to the cells of the human brain; but we must suppose that something similar occurs during nervous activity. Mental work exhausts the nerve-cells and they recover slowly."

The Consequent Effects of Fatigue on all Perceptions and Activities.—Direct observation upon man makes practically certain the foregoing conclusion of Dr. Burnham's. A postman, for example, can tell far more accurately in the morning than at night the weight of a letter. Our sense perceptions of all kinds are far acuter in the morning. It is literally true that the world looks brighter in the morning. The carefully observed results of fatigue in man all emphasize the wisdom of prompt heeding of the warnings of weariness, and the necessity of alternating periods of work and rest for both mental and moral health. Mosso's observations showed that "fatigue causes many strange phenomena: color-blindness, involuntary movements, hysterical symptoms, amorousness, hallucinations, prolonged after-images, and almost every kind of subjective and objective symptoms, suggesting the weaker parts of body or mind." The mental symptoms in normal fatigue, as noted by Dr. Cowles, are "loss of power of memory[1]; sense of perception less acute; association centers less spontaneous, and therefore slower[2]; the vocabulary diminishes; lowering of emotional tone; the attention unstable and flickering." These are the symptoms which the rational man ought to note as indicating that he is falling below his best, and he ought to plan to get back as promptly as possible to that best. The secret of the finest and the largest

[1] Corning says that the fluctuations of memory may be taken as a kind of barometer of the sanitary condition of the mind. *Brain Exhaustion*, p. 71.

[2] *Cf.* Royce, *Op. cit.*, p. 217.

work is to keep persistently at one's best. "Renewed power comes after rest and sleep." "But when the process of restoration is continuously incomplete, pathological fatigue or neurasthenia is the result."

Fatigue is, therefore, not merely physically uncomfortable; it is intellectually and morally dangerous, and it makes temptations possible that have cost many a man his character. The record of Saturday nights in this world of ours would make tragic reading. Germany may be said to have a practically national problem, that turns on the use of Saturday night. These facts help one to see why Mosso should insist that "the work done by a fatigued muscle (and the same law seems to hold for brain action) injures it far more than the same work under normal conditions"; for "half of a given quantity of work does not require half of a given time for rest." "A man's efficiency, then, depends upon his habits of mental thrift." Men evidently vary considerably in the promptness with which the nerve-cells recover from fatigue. Every man must find for himself his best periods of work and rest; but having found his individual law, he should remember that there is no gain but only loss in work undertaken contrary to that law.

In a word, self-control lies at the very basis of character, and of all achievement, intellectual or moral; the chief psychical condition of self-control is power of attention; attention is the chief factor in mental fatigue; the chief bodily condition of power of attention is, therefore, surplus nervous energy; and the conditions of surplus nervous energy are plain—food, rest, recreation, sleep, and especially avoidance of every species of excess, particularly emotional excess. And these conditions are largely within our control. Even sleep is largely under control of the will, and the world's best workers know this. Bodily conditions rightly observed can mightily help both intellectual and moral efficiency.

The religious life, least of all, with its belief in God as creator of both body and mind and expressing himself in their laws, can ignore these facts. While recognizing clearly that these are not all, nor the most important conditions, it will still, in subordination to the higher interests, be loyally obedient to these lesser laws. The spirit of obedience is best seen, often, in fidelity in the littles. How dear a price, in the spiritual life, has often been paid for the ignoring of this first plain physical condition of self-control!

We must persistently aim, then, at surplus nervous energy, at what Emerson calls "*plus health.*" And in no calling is this more imperative than in teaching, especially in the teaching of little children. It is the special prerogative of the child to see things freshly. If one is to be able to put himself at the child's point of view and see for him, one requires, above all, *freshness* — freshness of body, mind, and spirit. He must be neither strained nor fagged. This demands plus health. Dr. Munger makes the same suggestion for the ministry in the order of the words in the felicitous title of an important address to theological students, "*Health, Vitality, Inspiration.*"

"If ye know these things happy are ye if ye do them." As Dr. Gulick says of his "Ten Minutes' Exercise for Busy Men": "Exercise every day. If you don't you cannot say that *it* is a failure, *you* are the failure." Herbert Spencer, broken down with nervous exhaustion, made his farewell address to Americans on "The Gospel of Recreation."

Sydenham, author of a valuable treatise on gout, Lagrange says, "suffered from his first attack immediately on finishing his book." Knowing the truth, unfortunately, is not doing it.

Americans, especially, need Spencer's warnings, since no nation so persistently disregards these facts. For neurasthenia is a peculiarly American disease; some have even ventured to call it *Americanitis*. There are natural reasons for this condition, indeed, but they do not lessen the danger. One factor—that is at the same time both cause and symptom—is our nervous over-activity and tendency to repeated changes of occupation. But it should not be forgotten that this persistent disregard of nervous conditions both makes impossible our intellectual supremacy as a nation and increases enormously the difficulties of our moral problems. The greatest things cannot be possible to a people that is living on its nerves. Intellectual supremacy and moral leadership for a people requires *long-continued* labor on the part of many individuals. There is incalculable loss in the constant changing of intellectual leaders. We may well wonder if we are not attempting to live at a pace that gives us not only small time to think, but threatens seriously our power of normal feeling, our power to work, and our power to live righteously, to say nothing of our power greatly to lead in the highest things. Let us make it unmistakably clear to ourselves that no *fagged* man can be at his best. He dooms himself thereby to inferior work, inferior living, and inferior influence. If we are to see conditions normally, and face them with hope and courage, we need to escape fag.

The Need of Physical Training.—The psychical effects of bodily training, already referred to, are not only strong evidence of the influence of bodily conditions on mind and character, but urge most decisively the great importance of such training for the entire higher life of man. The effect of physical exercise upon organic feelings may be referred to here as an additional illustration of this importance; for, in Sully's words, "the organic feelings have a far-reaching effect on the higher emotional life."[1] The almost immediate effect of deep breathing in helping to do away with pathological fears is a closely related phenomenon.[2]

[1] *Op. cit.*, p. 477.
[2] *Cf.* James, *Op. cit.*, Vol. II, p. 459.

But there is another side of the matter. The close connection of body and mind means constant mutual interaction; not only the influence of the body on mind, but also the influence of mind on body.

II. THE INFLUENCE OF MIND ON BODY

Bodily conditions, correctly considered, must be viewed not as limitations, but as directions for the accomplishment of our ends, just as in the external world, we can accomplish our ends by observing nature's laws and fulfilling the implied conditions. There are conditions, but they may be made means of power. I have nothing to say here of the mysteries of Christian Science or metaphysical healing, or occultism in any of its forms, but mean to keep close to recognized scientific facts. For, as Professor Jastrow says, "the legitimate recognition of the importance of mental conditions in health and disease is one of the results of the union of modern psychology and modern medicine. An exaggerated and extravagant, as well as pretentious and illogical overstatement and misstatement of this principle, may properly be considered as occult."[1] The facts are, that

[1] *Fact and Fable in Psychology*, p. 26.

self-control is made vastly easier by right bodily conditions, and the normal way to self-control is through fulfilment of those conditions; but the mind may directly affect the body; and to the disciplined will, self-control is possible far beyond the limits of natural physical endurance. Bodily conditions are not omnipotent. "One of the most seductive and mischievous of errors," says Dr. Mortimer Granville, "is the practice of giving way to inertia, weakness, and depression. . . . Those who desire to live should settle this well in their minds, that nerve power is the force of life, and that the will has a wondrously strong and direct influence over the body, through the brain and nervous system."[1]

Power of Self-control even in the Insane.—The enormous power of self-control which even the insane (whose very condition is one of abnormal lack of self-control) are able at times to exert, is evidence of this fact. Thus, "a patient," Höffding relates, "once strove for twenty-seven years against hallucinations, which tempted him to attack others. Even his best friends suspected nothing until the day he declared himself vanquished and took

[1] Quoted by Lecky, *Op. cit.*, p. 18.

refuge in a lunatic asylum."[1] The result showed, of course, a long-continued and serious diseased condition; but the fact that that condition could be faced and mastered so long, shows what the will can do even in seriously abnormal conditions.

The Will in Determining Conditions of Health.—Moreover, the very beginning of improved nervous conditions often lies in the will itself, and in the will alone. Very much can be accomplished by persistent volition.

In Achieving Rest. — "Rest," Miss Brackett justly contends, "cannot be pasted on to one."[2] It is an active achievement. Rational living must often begin with a declaration of independence — a persistent lessening of one's pretensions — a steadfast refusal to undertake more than one can do without strain. For many of us there can be no rational living, except by a somewhat rigorous practice of Dr. Trumbull's "duty of refusing to do good." We have assumed too many duties that were not duties for us, and are attempting to do too many things at a time. The burden is never off, the strain

---

[1] *Outlines of Psychology*, p. 330. *Cf.* a similar case in James, *Op. cit.*, Vol. II, p. 542.

[2] *The Technique of Rest*, p. 19.

never remitted. We must resist "the devastator of the day." I am coming quite to believe in the almost inspired wisdom of an old "second reader" saw of my boyhood:

> "One thing at a time and that done well
> Is a very good rule, as many can tell;
> So work while you work, and play while you play,
> For that is the way to be cheerful and gay."

The poetry was not sublime, but the sense was good. The persistent practice of that principle made possible the enormous amount of work accomplished by Kingsley and still accomplishing by Edward Everett Hale.

In Avoiding Hurry.—*Haste* literally makes waste. Few things more certainly and thoroughly muddle the brain than a sense of hurry. One can work rapidly and still with complete self-possession and without hurry. But the peculiar sense of being hurried has a direct physical effect that may often be felt in the brain, and is distinctly confusing. To get on with one's work at all, one must often, by direct effort of the will, resist hurrying, recover his self-possession, and drive his work, instead of being driven by it. There is, sometimes, "possibility of great virtue in simply standing still." Work done in a hurry is work done poorly and at great loss. Miss Call quotes to the same effect Ruskin's "not great effort but great power," which recalls Dr. Bushnell's saying that, if he had his life to live over, he would "push less." This wearing sense of hurry, of effort, of push, is wholly within the power of one's will, and needs to be resisted especially by Americans.

In Meeting the Special Conditions of Surplus Nervous Energy.— Dr. Corning's rules for those of scanty mental reserve power enjoin avoidance of " (1) excessive emotion, (2) of frantic attempts to accomplish in one hour work appropriate to two, (3) of every species of excess which experience has proved leads to general constitutional drain, (4) of attempting to do two things at one and the same time, (5) of petty engagements which interfere with sleep." But every one of these rules calls for the exercise of will power. So do the positive conditions of surplus nervous energy already discussed.

In Control of the Emotions.— No single result of the study of nervous diseases seems to me more significant than that nerve specialists generally recognize, as one of the main factors in nervous health, the necessity of the *proper and habitual limitation of the emotions;* especially, Richardson says, "those most destructive passions—anger, hate, and fear," and worry may well be added to the list. "Brain-work," Dr. Granville says, "in the midst of worry is carried on in the face of ceaseless peril." And Miss Call lays special emphasis on the "nervous strain from sham emotions."[1] It is a specialist on brain exhaustion who writes, "Habits of consistent intellectual supervision of the emotions when once formed are one of the most precious acquisitions of life."[2] But this requires habitual volitional control in a particularly difficult field. It is possible, however, and not only mental health but bodily health requires it. The antithesis of this volitional self-control is letting oneself go, which means wreck— bodily and mental. But power of self-control is a fact, and a fact which physiological psychology makes as clear as bodily influence on the mind. No weakling can legitimately quote physiological psychology in his defense.

"*The physiological effect of faith*" is to be directly connected with this control of the emotions. As Dr. George E. Gorham says,[3]

[1] *Power Through Repose*, pp. 57 ff.
[2] Corning, *Brain Exhaustion*, p. 178.
[3] *The Outlook*, Aug. 19, 1899.

"the functional activities of the unconscious life are not under control of the will, save as the emotions are affected by will." "One cannot will the heart to cease or increase its regular beat. One cannot will that the process of digestion shall not go on." "The processes of unconscious life are under control of the sympathetic nervous system, and most of them go on independent of thought and unrecognized by it." As fear especially interferes with the normal on-going of these processes, so a faith that expels fear promotes them. "Suppose," Dr. Gorham says, "one comes into the presence of a sympathizing friend who excites all the ennobling emotions of love, trust, hope, and courage. None of the crippling effect of fear is in the body, but the whole life is stimulated by the faith and trust one has in the friend. Thoughts come quickly and freely. The body is at ease and its functions go on steadily and well. The unconscious processes of the body are only doing their best when they feel the throb of a great faith, a great hope, love and courage." By rational control of the emotions, thus, through putting ourselves in the presence of the great objective interests and personalities that naturally call out faith and hope and love, we may profoundly affect even the unconscious bodily functions. This means that control of the emotions must be indirect and objective, not direct and subjective.

And this suggests, what should be always in mind, that control of the body, like all self-control, must be positive in its method, not negative—fear and worry, for example, expelled by bringing in faith. This emphasis upon the necessary *positive character of self-control* is most important, especially in the emotional life, and will be more fully considered later.

III. MUTUAL INFLUENCE OF BODY AND MIND—HABITS

We have been considering phenomena, that led us to think now of the influence of body on mind, and now of the influence of mind on body; but the very idea of the unity of man in mind and body—the indissoluble way in which they are knit up together—indicates that the influence in every case is, at least, to some degree, mutual. Each constantly affects the other. And the phenomena of habit especially enforce this view. For, manifest as the physical basis of habit is, it is still a basis which it is quite possible for us to use in different lines, according to the direction of our attention. And, while there are natural time-limits in the formation of habits, within these limits we have the power to determine what our habits shall be. The nervous system simply comes in to second powerfully whatever we do, and to make it more certain that we shall do it again. The mind as certainly affects the body here, as the body the mind.

The Significance of Habit for Mental Life.— It surely is not necessary to dwell at length upon the significance of habit for the entire intellectual, moral, and spiritual life— its enormous hindrance or help throughout. Professor James puts the heart of the matter in these few sentences: "The great thing, then, in all education, is to make our nervous system our ally instead of our enemy. It is to fund and capitalize our acquisitions, and live at ease upon the interest of the fund. For this we must make automatic and habitual, as early as possible, as many useful actions as we can, and guard against the growing into ways that are likely to be disadvantageous to us, as we should guard against the plague. The more of the details of our daily life we can hand over to the effortless custody of automatism, the more our higher powers of mind will be set free for their own proper work."[1]

We are not likely to give too earnest heed to the law of habit, with its physical basis, in facing the problem of living. To forget these facts of habit may be to leave our whole higher life to darkness and defeat. Increasingly we must be able to hand over to habit earlier and lower problems, that we may give ourselves the more fully to the deepening problems of the spiritual life. And that this is often not done is one of the fruitful causes of small attainment in the higher ranges of our being.

James also brings home with a vividness that cannot be escaped, the certainty with which habit works in the various spheres of our life. "Every smallest stroke of virtue or of vice leaves its never so little scar. The drunken Rip Van Winkle, in Jefferson's play, excuses himself for every fresh dereliction by saying, 'I won't count this time.' Well! he may not count it, and a kind Heaven may not count it; but it is being counted none

[1] *Psychology*, Vol. I, p. 122.

the less. Down among the nerve-cells and fibers the molecules are counting it, registering and storing it up, to be used against him when the next temptation comes. Nothing we ever do is, in strict scientific literalness, wiped out. Of course this has its good side as well as its bad one. As we become permanent drunkards by so many separate drinks, so we become saints in the moral, authorities and experts in the practical and scientific spheres, by so many separate acts and hours of work. Let no youth have any anxiety about the upshot of his education, whatever the line of it may be. If he keep faithfully busy each hour of the working-day, he may safely leave the final result to itself."[1]

Opportunities for Will Training in Formation of Habits in Education.— And one can hardly help emphasizing here the great opportunities of will training, in the formation of good habits, that his educational environment affords the student. The person who means to grow, we have seen, must, as early as possible, "make automatic and habitual as many useful habits as he can." And the opportunity for this, quite apart from all intellectual advantage, is enough to make one's

[1] *Op. cit.*, Vol. I, p. 127.

student days priceless. Let the college student, for example, face his environment, not to chafe under it or against it, but to submit himself loyally to its discipline, or rather to discipline himself under it, and he will have no reason to complain of the result. Here is opportunity — but only opportunity — for training to those conditions of surplus nervous energy that guard the sources of one's best mental work, to promptness in meeting engagements and promptness in work, to constancy and perseverance in work, to that "patience that is almost power," to superiority to moods — working because the work is to be done, and not because one feels like it, to regularity and system in work, to self-control and self-denial, to absolute honesty with oneself and others as against the fatal facility in making excuses, to power of attention, to simple will-power. It is a great opportunity to learn steady fidelity; but it is only an opportunity. Zeller was one of the greatest historians of philosophy, but Zeller said with manifest pride, when he laid down his work in the University of Berlin, that for eighty semesters he had not omitted a single lecture.

One point deserves special emphasis —

the great danger or the great opportunity for will training, in the multiplied occasions in one's educational life, which call for *attention*. The habits of continuous inattention which some students form in recitation, lecture, and church service are nothing short of deadly. I am not likely to speak too strongly here. The power of attention is the very center of will. Habits of continuous inattention and mind-wandering, therefore, mean the sapping of the sources of will-power. It is largely one's own miserable inattention which makes it possible for him to speak so contemptuously of what he hears; but were all he says true, it would still be a gigantic wrong against himself to use these occasions only to tear himself down. There are times, no doubt, when one's bodily presence is required on an occasion, but when his condition makes it unwise to attempt close attention. At such times, one should guard himself against habits of inattention by deliberately settling it with himself that he is not now to attend, and makes no attempt to do so. But if one is intending to attend, let him attend.

James' Maxims on Habit.—For the rest, Professor James has made this subject of habit so much his own by his incomparable chapter on the subject, that one is almost forced to quote from him his statement of the maxims for the forming of new habits or the breaking of old, without which any discussion of habit for practical ends would be quite incomplete.

(1) Launch yourself with "as strong and decided an initiative as possible. Accumulate all the possible circumstances which shall reinforce the right motives; put yourself assiduously in conditions that encourage the new way; make engagements incompatible with the old; take a public pledge, if the case allows; in short, envelope your resolution with every aid you know." To similar import, John Foster, in his famous essays, *On Decision of Character*, says: "If once his judgment is really decided, let him commit himself irretrievably, by doing something which shall oblige him to do more, which shall lay on him the necessity of doing all." This is really to cross the Rubicon, to burn behind one every bridge that may allow any way of retreat from his purpose, and to burn his boats as well.

(2) The second maxim is: "Never suffer an exception to occur until the new habit

is securely rooted in your life. Each lapse is like the letting fall of a ball of string which one is carefully winding up; a single slip undoes more than a great many turns will wind again." Nathan Sheppard gives a characteristic illustration of this maxim, when he says to public speakers: "Dash cold water on the throat every morning when you wash, for 365, not 364, mornings of the year."

(3) "Seize the very first possible opportunity to *act* on every resolution you make, and on every emotional prompting you may experience in the direction of the habits you aspire to gain." It is *action* alone that fixes the habit. "Let the expression," James adds, "be the least thing in the world — speaking genially to one's grandmother, or giving up one's seat in a horse-car, if nothing more heroic offers — but let it not fail to take place."

(4) "Keep the faculty of effort alive in you by a little gratuitous exercise every day. That is, be systematically ascetic or heroic in little unnecessary points, do every day or two something for no other reason than that you would rather not do it, so that when the hour of dire need draws nigh, it may find you not unnerved and untrained to

stand the test." Daily inure yourself "to habits of concentrated attention, energetic volition, and self-denial in unnecessary things."[1]

IV. THE TRUE PLACE OF ASCETICISM

This last maxim of James may sound, to some alert Protestant, too Catholic, too much like an advocacy of the doctrine of the virtue of self-sacrifice for its own sake, of judging that a thing is "your duty because you hate it so." Yet the advice is, I believe, on the whole, so sound and so important, that it leads one to ask, What is the truth as to asceticism? The religious life, especially, has always recognized its necessary connection with the body, in its attempt to solve this question of asceticism. For this reason, too, therefore, in considering the bodily conditions of true living, one can hardly shirk a frank facing of the vexed question, What is the true place of asceticism? Has it a rightful place at all? Has the Protestant reaction from the Catholic position here been extreme? Has the "new Puritanism" lost something of the strength of the old?

[1] *Psychology*, Vol. I, pp. 122–127.

The Body Not Evil Per se.—In the first place, we can probably agree that asceticism is not to be defended so far as it is based upon the belief that matter and body are evil *per se*, and opposed to the life of the spirit. We are not Parsees nor Manichæans. Abuse of the body can help no virtue. Disregarding nervous conditions which are a part of God's own ordainment cannot help to obedience in other things. It was this aspect of asceticism, that seems to delight in limitation for its own sake, which Goethe so abhorred and which he so constantly fought. The Gospel gives no sanction to the principle that the good things of life are from the devil rather than from God. But still it understands clearly that bodily goods are subordinate and relative.

Obviously, the demands of duty in a given case may require the complete subordination of bodily interests, even of any possible health; but in no case is this to be recklessly assumed; and even where it is necessary, it is still a manifest evil, and gives no excuse for any voluntary abuse of the body. Any asceticism that lowers bodily vitality is just so far not a help but a hindrance to self-control. The only safe asceticism is one that makes us more, not less, careful of the conditions of the highest bodily health. As President Stanley Hall says, "Even will training does not reach its end till it leads the young up to taking an intelligent, serious and life-long interest in their own physical culture and development."[1] A true asceticism, then, may not fight the body, as evil *per se*.

Asceticism, as Negative, No Full Goal of Life.—We may, perhaps, also agree, in the second place, that asceticism can never be the price of any real salvation or that salvation itself. Necessarily negative, it cannot furnish in itself a positive goal of abundant life. This was the view against which the Reformers warred, and which Paul characterized as only a "show of wisdom." Asceticism is not a good in itself; at its best it is good only as means, as moral gymnastic. No rational being can take pleasure in pain as such, or regard asceticism as at all meeting the requirements of virtue. One might go the whole length of the most absolute asceticism, and not yet have begun to love. The preëminent importance of self-control to the moral life, it should be noted, lies not in itself, nor in the mere casting off of the lower goods, but in its making possible the

[1] *Pedagogical Seminary*, Vol. II, p. 75.

positive attainment of the greater goods, for the sake of which the lower are sacrificed. It looks to growth, to the constantly enlarging life.

Moreover, it should not be forgotten that, psychologically, self-control itself, in spite of its seemingly negative name, is always positive; though the vast army of ascetics have too often overlooked this fact, and so have failed the more disastrously. We conquer the tempting thought only by positively replacing it by something else. No man has attained real freedom from the domination of evil or from the domination of the lesser goods, until a sense of the great realities and values has taken hold upon him. The deliverance which the Gospel seeks is always of this positive kind, not merely negative. Mere flight from the world is cowardly, narrow, selfish, and self-contradictory. To cut oneself off from all possible relations can be no good training to a love that involves relations. Life is far richer and more complex than an ascetic morality can ever know. We are to be in the world, though not of the world.

Not Two Kinds of Christianity.—Once more, in this attempt to determine the true place of asceticism, we must be on our guard that we do not virtually fall back into the self-contradictory, despairing solution of Catholicism, to which Harnack calls attention, which, while teaching "that it is only in the form of monasticism that true Christian life finds its expression," still "admits a 'lower' kind of Christianity without asceticism as 'sufficient.'"[1] There is a subtle temptation which besets us here. When we speak of taking on what we call unnecessary self-denials, of being rigorous with ourselves in "unnecessary" things; when we hunt out for ourselves "unnecessary" sacrifices, not naturally involved in the highest conception of our duty, are we not really adopting this old idea of two kinds of Christianity, and creating again the notion of works of supererogation, outside of what could be rightly required of us, and upon which, therefore, we may justly pride ourselves? The ambiguity of that word "unnecessary," it is to be feared, makes possible here a quite mistaken over-estimation of asceticism and so, of course, an entire misconception of its true place.

In what sense are these proposed measures of self-discipline "unnecessary"? Unnecessary, truly, in the sense that they are

[1] *What is Christianity*, p. 79.

not compelled by circumstances or by the will of another; unnecessary also, perhaps, in the sense that another, looking over the situation, would not feel justified in laying these things upon us as duties; but not unnecessary in the sense that *we* did not feel that, for the sake either of others or of our own later higher efficiency and victory, we would better do them. We believed they had a real and valuable contribution to make, either to ourselves or to others, and therefore we did them. If this was not true, and no one was to gain in any degree by our small asceticisms, if they had positively no contribution to make, then they were in truth not only unnecessary, but utterly valueless and unreasonable, without justification of any kind, except on the doctrine that the painful is to be chosen for its own sake, that a thing is a duty simply because one hates it so. From either point of view, it must be seen that asceticism, as self-discipline, is no reason for great pride. For, as Pfleiderer remarked in one of his lectures, this is only to be proud of one's need of discipline, since the only rational justification of asceticism is that one needs it.

In truth, in ingeniously hunting out these

new, supposedly "unnecessary" and supererogatory spheres of "will-worship," have men not with practical uniformity left behind many plain common duties? They have at best but tithed the mint and anise and caraway-seed, and have left undone the weightier matters of the law, justice, and mercy, and faith.[1] Are we sure that there are any such "unnecessary" valuable exercises? And, if there are, are not most of us so far in arrears in those countless opportunities of plainly valuable self-sacrifices for others, and in equally plainly needed self-disciplines for ourselves, that we may dismiss the question as purely academic—never occurring in actual life?

The True Asceticism.—Abandoning, then, all idea of some separate, superior virtue of "unnecessary" asceticism, we may still feel that there is a real place, and a psychological basis and need for a personal, private, humble, unblinded, sweet, and reasonable mental and moral hygiene, which is at the same time quite consistent with bodily hygiene, and which Paul advised, when he said, "So run that ye may obtain." "All things are lawful for me; but all things are

[1] Matt. 23:23.

not expedient. All things are lawful for me; but I will not be brought under the power of any." Paul's principle is that final victory requires self-control, all along the way; that those conditions, above all, must be fulfilled that mean winning in the race. And that will mean holding in stern abeyance the appetites and passions, and the giving up often of many pleasant things. The relative goods are nowhere to be allowed to jeopardize the highest goods.

But to get a shattered nervous system, and thin and vitiated blood, we may be sure, is no "laying aside every weight." The true aim should be to make one's body the best possible instrument, medium, and foundation for the spirit — to seek not only the "grace of a blameless body," but the grace of a positively helpful body. And this is no lackadaisical purpose. It takes far less will to violate the conditions of health in the doing of worthy work, than to fulfil them, as the number of manifestly fagged men in places of responsibility shows. And few things are a severer test or better training of the will-power of a man than fidelity to this trust of his body. To be truly temperate and fully to meet the requirements of health of body gives an ample field for will training — an ampler field, it is to be feared, than most of us are cultivating.

But for the sake of body and mind — for the very existence of a true spiritual life — we shall never be set free from fighting against what John Rae regards as the peculiar temptation of our time, — "*the passion for material comfort.*" In spite of grievous mistakes, the long history of asceticism has been right in its fundamental protest, — that the greatest things of the spirit cannot come to the ease-loving and self-indulgent, and that no price is too great to pay for the attainment of the highest. Bishop Westcott's suggestion in his posthumous book, that, though we were not to return to a confraternity of monks, we might well look to confraternities of families pledged to plain living and high thinking, at least points out one of the gravest dangers of our time for a rigorous spiritual life. And asceticism will always find its true place in the steady fight to maintain all the positive bodily conditions of the highest spiritual life, and rigorously to subordinate the lower goods to the highest. That much, we may be sure, is needed all along the line.

Our study of the unity of mind and body seems, then, to make it clear that, for the sake of the higher interests themselves, we may not neglect the body. Browning's words come to us, thus, not as a skeptical question, but as an inspiring challenge:

> "To man, propose this test—
> Thy body at its best,
> How far can that project thy soul on its lone way?"

But psychology's emphasis on the unity of man means not only the unity of mind and body, but also the special unity of the mind in all its functions.

CHAPTER VII

THE UNITY OF THE MIND — THE PSYCHOLOGICAL EVIDENCE

MODERN psychologists agree in emphasizing the unity of the mind. Insistence on the interdependence of all the phases of the mind has become, indeed, one of the commonplaces of the schools, and is one of the chief points of difference from the older psychology. Isolated faculties are denied.

I. INTERDEPENDENCE OF ALL INTELLECTUAL FUNCTIONS

It is recognized that no hard and fast lines can be drawn between the various intellectual activities, that each activity involves the germ of the later developing activities, and that there is always reciprocal aid. Judgment and inference, for example, are seen to be already active in the simplest perception. The danger of all exclusive tendencies is felt. Starr can even say: "All imperfect educational methods which hinder an harmonious development of mental traits and fail to develop character, act as predisposing causes to insanity."[1] Every activity must have its appropriate development for the sake of the whole. Thus Sully says: "An eye uncultivated in a nice detection of form means a limitation of all after-knowledge. Imagination will be hazy, thought loose and inaccurate where the preliminary stage of perception has been hurried over." So, too, as to thinking and imagining, "even when the concepts have been properly formed, they can only be kept distinct, and consequently accurate, by going back again and again to the concrete objects, out of which they have, in a manner, been extracted." "Thinking is not the same thing as imagining, yet it is based on it and cannot safely be divorced from it."[2]

Royce says still more broadly: "Sensory experience plays its part, and its essential part, in the very highest of our spiritual existence.

---
[1] *Diseases of the Mind*, p. 46.
[2] *Op. cit.*, pp. 213, 372.

These two inferences, it may be said in passing, constitute a considerable part of the psychological basis of the kindergarten. In training both the senses and the imagination, it should also be noticed, room should be left for a child's own imagination, freedom and activity. A rag-baby, thus, may be better than a full-fledged French doll.— *Cf.* Sully, *Op. cit.*, p. 215.

When we wish to cultivate processes of abstract thinking, our devices must, therefore, include a fitting plan for the cultivation of the senses, and must not seek to exclude sense experience as such, but only to select among sensory experiences those that will prove useful for a purpose." "Whatever be the best form of religious training, *it ought deliberately to make use of a proper appeal to the senses.*"[1] Even modern logic follows here the trend of psychology, and refuses to isolate abstractly the processes of conception, judgment, and inference, or even the processes of induction and deduction; it demands, instead, the recognition of the organic unity and continuity of all thinking.[2]

Indeed, modern psychology may be said to affirm that the intellect has but one fundamental function—the discernment of relationship. The one supreme counsel—consider relations—is counsel to fulfil every mental function: concentrated attention, assimilation, discrimination, selection, and synthesis. For concentrated attention requires considering an object in its varied aspects and relations; assimilation is only seeing the relations of like-

---

[1] *Op. cit.*, pp. 128, 129.
[2] *Cf.* Bowne, *Theory of Thought and Knowledge*, p. iii, e. g.

ness; discrimination, those of difference; selection is choosing out the more significant relations; and synthesis is but putting things in their relations to the whole. And it is by exactly these processes that we come to the mastery of any situation. To consider a thing in all its relations, it should be noted, moreover, carries with it deliberation, self-control, and open-mindedness, and is the secret of complete mental wakefulness. This is, then, in truth, not only the supreme intellectual counsel, but counsel for all living:—Consider relations. Our mistakes, in every line, are made through failing to preadjust attention, thought, or words to the coming circumstances, overlooking some vital bearing of the matter in hand—forgetting some relation. What a recognition is this, both of the unity of the mind itself, and of its inevitable search for unity.

II. INTERDEPENDENCE OF INTELLECT, FEELING AND WILL

Modern psychologists are also agreed on the complete interdependence of intellect, feeling, and will; that they are, in fact, never separated; that pure feeling, pure willing, and pure thinking are abstractions; that the whole mind acts in each; that there is, for example, no thought without some accompanying feeling, and some impulse to action. So Royce speaks of "the persistent stress that I lay upon the unity of the intellectual and the voluntary processes, which, in popular treatises, are too often sundered and treated as if one of them could go on without the other."[1] This insistence cannot legitimately be made to mean that these three phases of the mind's life can be reduced to any one of the three; they cannot be said in strict necessary logic to involve one another; but so great is the real unity of the mind that, as a simple matter of fact, each phase is always accompanied by some activity of the other phases. The whole mind always acts.[2] This is a commonplace of modern psychology, but of great practical significance. Now, this insistence upon unity even as regards these three great phases of the mind, logically carries with it, and with even greater reason, its full admission elsewhere. If even these may not be separated, there is still less legitimacy in analyzing a single activity into mere elements.

[1] *Op. cit.*, p. viii.
[2] *Cf.* Lotze, *The Microcosmus*, Vol. I, pp. 178–180.

III. TREND TOWARD THE DENIAL OF ABSTRACT ELEMENTS IN THE MIND

And it is perhaps not too much to say, in spite of the real differences between schools of psychology upon just this point, that the keynote of much of the best and latest work in psychology — and that of more than one school — has been the revolt against the extreme individualism — the abstract atomism — which began with Berkeley and Hume; and a demand for a recognition of something more than a sum of elements in mental processes, if we are really to meet the actual concrete facts and make knowledge possible at all.[1] This consideration will occupy us more fully later, in the treatment of the fourth great inference from modern psychology.

IV. THE MIND'S CONSTANT SEARCH FOR UNITY

In most significant harmony with this trend of modern psychology, is the result of Lotze's painstaking inquiry in the *Microcosmus*,[2] for the distinguishing characteristic

[1] *Cf.* James, *Op. cit.*, Vol. I, Chap. IX; Bowne, *Theory of Thought and Knowledge*, Part I, Chapters II and III.
[2] Vol. I, Book V.

of the human mind. This distinguishing endowment he finds in this very vision of unity, the power everywhere to see a whole, the capacity of endless progress toward the Infinite. The characteristic of human sense-perception, he believes, is that every content has its place in a whole, and its intrinsic excellence as a part of that whole; human language, he argues, bears the impress of a universal order; human intelligence has a clear consciousness of one universal truth; and man has, besides, an ineradicable sense of duty that leads to a yet higher unity of the entire personal world. The unity of the mind itself is evidenced here, again, by its inevitable recognition of unity everywhere. James, even in the discussion of the perception of space, speaks of "an ultimate law of our consciousness," "that we simplify, unify, and identify as much as we possibly can." It is this insatiable thirst of the mind for unity, which shows itself at its highest in the scientific and in the philosophic spirit, with their attempts to think the world through into unity. This deep trend of the mind may surely be taken as legitimate evidence of its own unity. And this unity will come out still more clearly in the concrete facts involved in the practical suggestions which follow.

In general, this recognition of the unity of the mind implies that there are psychical as well as physical conditions of growth, of character, of happiness, and of influence. "There is a mental, just as much as a bodily hygiene," Höffding says.[1]

[1] *Outlines of Psychology*, p. 333.

CHAPTER VIII

THE UNITY OF THE MIND—SUGGESTIONS FOR LIVING

IN general, the unity of the mind implies that there should be no ignoring of the psychical conditions of living; but rather, a practical recognition of the interdependence of all the mental functions. It means that one may not use or treat his mind as made up of independent parts; that it is a vain delusion to think that one can toy with cynical opinions, and leave feeling and will still humane and sympathetic; that he can indulge in false emotions, and keep thought true and conduct unflecked; that he can choose against reason, and not give his inner creed a twist, and not betray his deepest feeling. It means, on the other hand, that there can be no earnest and persistent search for the truth, that shall not blossom in truer and more delicate feeling, and fruit in nobler action; that to have done once for all with wrong feeling and sham emotions, brings more genuine insight into truth, and greater loyalty to it; that one cannot take upon him life's supreme choices and not feel more deeply and think more clearly. It means that defeat in one sphere tends to defeat in all; but that conquest in one helps to conquest in all. It means that we may and must steadily *count* upon the unity of the mind.

In particular, this unity of the mind implies that all true living has its *intellectual, emotional, and volitional conditions*. And it is no idle inquiry to ask how our thinking and feeling and choosing may affect our growth, whether in character, in happiness, or in influence. The most earnest-minded of all generations — Socrates, Paul, Augustine, Luther, — have felt that life was a battle, its fiercest and most critical engagements fought wholly within, with no observer to register the victory or defeat save God and the soul. With calm exterior, perhaps even with the every-day commonplaces on his lips, one may have seemed to go his usual way, while still within him there was waged a mortal combat. What is this inner battlefield, where man fights alone? What are our available forces, what our most dangerous foes? This is the meaning of a careful inquiry into the intellectual, emotional, and volitional conditions of true living.

The volitional conditions will be dealt with in the consideration of the third great inference from psychology—the central importance of will and action. The present chapter is confined to the treatment of some of the more important intellectual and emotional conditions of sane and righteous living.

I. THE INTELLECTUAL CONDITIONS

The very idea of intellectual conditions of true living implies that the habits of our thinking may either help or hinder us in our attainment of character and happiness and influence. And the relation of thinking to living may be, perhaps, made most clear by noting both the ways in which habits of thought may help, and the ways in which they may hinder life.

Intellectual Helps.—The conviction of the unity of the mind forces us to believe that, if the mind is rightly trained in its intellectual functions, that training will contribute to the whole life. Right thinking affects the mind in most subtle and deep-going ways.

H

In the first place, as has already been pointed out, it must not be forgotten that wise conduct of life is greatly furthered by the possession of a considerable *circle of permanent interests*, of a "store of stable and worthy ends," that enlarge and deepen life, that make it sane and wholesome, that give some opportunity for freedom of choice, that continually serve both as standards of value, and as effective motives to action, and that give a man secure anchorage in time of storm. It must be one of the chief aims of education to give us such permanent interests. More need not be said upon this here[1].

In the second place, it must be manifest that a prime condition of steady growth into one's highest life is *knowledge of oneself*—rational taking account of one's own temperament and tendencies and powers. One can hardly handle himself to best advantage if he does not thoroughly understand himself, especially his prevailing temperament. There is an old proverb which says that at forty every man is either a fool or a physician. And it holds for the mind as well as for the body. We ought to know ourselves and the conditions of our best living.

[1] *Cf.* above, pp. 9 ff.

Is one's *temperament* predominantly intellectual, or emotional, or volitional? It concerns him to know and to guard himself accordingly. The predominantly intellectual man is likely to find it almost impossible to fulfil some of the chief conditions of sympathy, and so to cut himself off from his fellows, to narrow his own life, to jeopardize his character, and to limit both his happiness and his influence. The predominantly emotional man is likely to relapse into simple sentimentalism, that neither thinks clearly nor puts the feeling into act; while the predominantly volitional man may attain merely an unreasoning, unfeeling obstinacy. "Woe to the man," says Murray, "who cultivates energy of will without the guidance of reason or without the amenity of genial sentiment."[1] So, too, for guidance in conduct, one needs to ask, in the intellectual sphere, Do I merely *see* things, or have I learned also really to think them? As to feeling, is it the physical or the ideal that most appeals to me, the egoistic or the sympathetic? Am I most affected by pleasure or by pain? As to will, am I naturally impulsive or resolute? Is expression difficult

[1] *Education of Will, Educational Review*, Vol. II, pp. 57 ff.

or easy for me? If difficult, is it from excessive inhibition—the danger of Northern peoples—or from defective impulse? Well-warranted reserve may pass into practical inability to express our love for others at all. If expression is for me easy, is it from weak inhibition—the danger of Southern peoples—or from strong impulse?[1] The method to be pursued in remedying the defect in one's character, it is evident, must be very different in the different cases. And, in general, do I react strongly and quickly, or strongly and slowly, weakly and quickly, or weakly and slowly?

So, again, men differ greatly in their natural estimate of themselves. Some, of course, habitually overestimate themselves; others—perhaps, on the whole, quite as numerous a class—are as habitually self-depreciative. Both need to take account of their tendency, if they are to live wisely and happily. Occasionally a man needs soberly and deliberately to form the habit of adding fifty per cent to his natural estimate of what he means to his friends. He is continually losing power and happiness through an underestimate of his own significance. The blunders of the self-conceited are even more obvious.

[1] *Cf.* James, *Op. cit.*, Vol. II, pp. 537 ff, 546 ff.

Dangers and temptations plainly vary with temperament. As a single example, it is easy to see that it is well for a man to take account of his temperament as to the *kind of memories* he has; for these come in directly to affect decision. It is a psychological fact that some men have good memories for joys and successes, and poor memories for injuries and sorrows and difficulties. Of others, the reverse is true. The former are apt to be rash in their decisions and undertakings; the latter to find both positive decision and undertaking difficult. Note, for example, the bearing of these kinds of memory upon the duty of forgiveness. Some of us simply cannot recall after a time how mean a man has been to us; we cannot reproduce with any vividness the original situation; it is comparatively easy for such to forgive. Others can bring back the whole scene in detail, and powerfully feel it again; for such, forgiveness is much harder.

It should need no argument to prove, in particular, that this forgetting of differences of temperament is a most fruitful cause of the seeming unreality of the spiritual life. Men question their own spiritual insights and experiences because these do not come to them in the same way as those of others of quite different temperaments. Both need to take account of their temperaments, when decisions are to be made.

More definitely, the intellect may help character, by giving a *clear discernment of what moral progress is*. Even this, however, is plainly not a purely intellectual problem, but a part of our moral conflict itself. But the intellect may contribute much. Even if it were true that a man's purpose at a given time were wholly right, yet progress would be possible to him. Clear thinking may show that progress is possible in steadiness of purpose, in the multiplication of motives to insure the persistent purpose, and in broader, deeper, more skilful and delicate application of the purpose. In the first place, growing insight should place before a man so clearly and completely the different relations of his purpose to the well-being of himself and of others, as to put almost beyond desire any opposite course; and the flickering, vacillating will becomes thus replaced by unshaken steadiness of purpose.

Progress is also possible in the *broader* application of the right purpose. Nearly all men live in more or less constant blindness to certain spheres of moral conduct. In certain relations, the moral problem is never raised. The knights of the Middle Ages, for example, were, many of them, men of genuine and chivalrous Christian purpose, yet few recognized any large duty to their poorest dependents. One awakes at times with a kind of amazement to the recognition of a duty that has long stared him squarely in the face, but which nevertheless for him has not previously seemed to exist. Much of our moral growth consists in the broadening application of well-recognized principles, in the widening of the field of obligation. The awakening of our own generation to a new social consciousness is a marked example of such broadening of the moral life.

But great progress is possible as well in the *deeper* application of the right purpose. Here belongs the growing discernment of the rich complexity and significance of life, of the destiny of man, of the worth of personality and of personal relations — a discernment that makes a man's previous aims and achievements seem shallow and imperfect enough. Life means so much more to him, that his sense of obligation has deepened proportionately. He cannot treat lightly his own life, or the life of another.

And to come to such a sense of the sacredness of life's calling, is at the same time to see the possible progress in *more skilful and delicate* application of the right purpose. Real tact implies moral advancement. One longs for an imagination more creative and profound, to present to himself adequately the circumstances of the other man; a judgment more delicately sensitive to discern the precise forms in which his purpose should now be embodied. Such judgment and such imagination are no happy inheritance; they come only from long moral experience and discipline. It is this skilful and delicate application which makes the highest attainment in morals — real beauty of character — the ideal embodiment of one's ideal — possible.

But the most direct intellectual help to a wise conduct of life comes from *clearness and definiteness in memory, imagination, and thinking*. To remember with distinctness the entire and exact consequences of previous experiences, to be able to set before oneself with vivid and detailed imagination even the remote results of the action now contemplated—this is to be able to call to one's aid the strongest motives to righteousness. Clear and definite thinking, moreover, moves directly and unhesitatingly toward its goal, and for that very reason seems to be a distinct help to decisive action. For all purposeful action involves the use of definite means to definite ends. Definiteness in thinking, thus, seems to be directly connected with decision in action, and vagueness of thinking with indecision and weakness.

It is therefore of great moral value to form a habit of requiring of oneself clearness and definiteness with reference to all with which one means seriously to deal—clearness and definiteness in the original impressions, in memories, in insights, in purposes, in statements. There must be no suffering of oneself in vague reasonings, vague bargains, vague promises, and vague conclusions. When decision and definiteness are at all possible, there should be a complete avoidance of all vagueness and procrastination, and a firm purpose to look the facts fully in the face. Intellectual vagueness is a habit easy to form, and bodily weariness greatly favors it; but it is a habit distinctly inimical to the acquirement of will-power and of practical power to act. It can be conquered only by a positive cultivation of the opposite habit of clearness and definiteness in the entire intellectual life.

Lotze shows some of the broader implications of this principle in a suggestive passage, that is well worth quoting at length: "To a character of thorough moral development every entangled complication of circumstances, every uncertainty regarding claims which it is entitled to make or called upon to satisfy, every doubt about its relation to others, is as odious as bodily impurity. We need only compare with this the prevailing inclinations of the lower classes, in order to see those moral deficiencies which it is so hard for imperfect civilization to avoid; the difficulty of extracting from them a definite, decided promise, their constant disposition to leave everything they can in a state of fluctuating uncertain indecision, their inaccessibility to the notion that one's word once given is of binding obligation, and — in wider circles — the propensity to cling to doubtful and untenable relations, the hope that if one never takes a decided step one will be able in the hurly-burly of events to snatch some advantage, of which one has at present no clear notion — in short, inexhaustible patience with all sorts of confusion, and a delight in wriggling on, with the help of procrastination, waiting about, half-admissions and retractions, and general uncertainty, through the course of events which to men thus inclined seems itself equally uncertain."[1] "Among the more intelligent upper classes the same deficiency recurs, but under other forms, or under the same forms, but in different connections; among them, as among those whose conditions of life are less favored, the noble spirits are but few, but there are some of these in all ranks of life—souls who, with an unwearied impulse toward truth, renounce all those pretexts with which the slothful of heart seek to excuse this mental instability, and who, moved by the enthusiasm and force of moral conviction, not only desire to make their whole duty clear before their eyes at every step of this changing life, but also obey with unhesitating decision every clear call to action."[2] "I kept guarding," says Augustine, "in my inner perception the

[1] The character of Chilo in *Quo Vadis* is an admirable example of this type.
[2] *The Microcosmus*, Vol. II, p. 63.

integrity of my perceptions; and in the trifling thoughts which are suggested by trifling things, I was delighted in the truth."[1]

Intellectual Hindrances.—These very illustrations make it clear that intellectual habits may hinder as well as help true living.

And, first, it is possible to cultivate *intellectual conditions that fairly paralyze the will*. Premature multiplication of points of view, the attitude of merely curious inquiry—"truth-hunting," as Augustine Birrell calls it—the simply questioning spirit, the purely reflective and morbidly introspective mind, as well as playing with cynicism and pessimism—all bring weakness of will and defective character. We may well press Birrell's pertinent inquiry: "Are you sure that it is a good thing for you to spend so much time in speculating about matters outside your daily life and walk?" "Nothing so much tends to obliterate plain duties as the free indulgence of speculative habits." "The verdict to be striven for is not 'well-guessed,' but 'well-done.'"[2] Stanley Hall feels this so strongly that he says that philosophy may be so taught as to "produce nothing less than a

[1] Quoted by Granger, *The Soul of the Christian*, p. 263.
[2] *Obiter Dicta*, Essay on *Truth-hunting*.

morbid neurosis of cynicism, indifference, and selfishness."[1] And even Royce says: "Philosophy is most decidedly not for everybody."

It was a sound instinct which led Descartes, in his attempt to follow to the bitter end the significance of a universal though "provisional doubt," to adopt, meanwhile, a definite code of morals which should control him in this skeptical period. There may easily be premature philosophizing that reacts disastrously on conduct; since only deeper thinking and longer experience can make clear how deeply laid are the foundations of moral principles. For, as one of the greatest philosophers of our generation has said, "The dignity of any moral custom or ceremony can very seldom be convincingly shown when it is regarded in isolation, and not in its connection with the whole spiritual significance of human life; having a thousand roots entwined in this, it is generally wholly incapable of a concise syllogistic proof that does not, in its turn, require to have its own presuppositions supported by an infinite series of proof. Just on this account every moral command is exposed to destructive sophistry."[2] That is, the very

[1] In article on *The New Psychology, as a Basis of Education*.
[2] Lotze, *The Microcosmus*, Vol. II, p. 54.

depth and significance of the proof expose it the more to shallow attack.

It is of no small value here to keep one's feet planted firmly on the ground, to keep in touch with sensible objects, to work — actually to work — upon things; we cannot easily become sophists when we are in normal, actual contact with things. This is a part of the value of the message of Tolstoi and Howells. The fact that something is actually being brought to pass shows that one is dealing with real things and real forces, and not simply with his own speculations. Cæsar's enthusiastic pride in his own bridge-building, Carlyle's admiration of his father's bridges, and Stevenson's elation in his vegetables may have here, in part, at least, their psychological explanation.

Too few remember that the function of doubt — by the very make-up of our nature — is always only temporary, provisional; that the true opposite of belief, as another has said, is not disbelief, which means only another belief, but doubt, which paralyzes action; that belief is the only normal state. Robust disbelief is one thing; but incessant quibbling, analyzing, subtilizing, playing dilettante, sceptic, and sophist, is quite another. What sense of reality can there be for such minds, what truth, what reverence, what enthusiasm, or what purpose? Mighty purposes are born of mighty convictions, and not otherwise. No wonder that Charles Wagner rings out over the youth of France: "Enough of negations, enough, above all, of jugglers and *poseurs!* Give us men of faith and action, of love and hate, with a clear seeing eye, a breast that throbs, and a vigorous arm; men who, emancipated from idle fancies and the empty din of words, are silent, and putting their hands to the plow, drive, as their witness, a straight furrow in the field of life."[1]

Yet, it is probable that just here lies the danger of the highly educated man. The very breadth of view which his education has brought, the capacity to see many aspects of a matter, his cultivated emphasis on the many-sidedness of truth — all tend to "*over-sophistication*." A fatal facility in taking any point of view or of defending any proposition, which is one of the natural products of his education, carries with it the danger of breaking down all real conviction. And so it is quite possible for a man to graduate

[1] Charles Wagner, *Youth*, p. 67.

from college with high honors, but positively less fitted for any valuable and effective work in life than if he had never seen college doors.

Nothing can replace in value the great fundamental convictions. And yet it is a mistaken inference to make breadth of view a denial of all depth of view — to make many-sidedness of truth a reason for giving up truth. Breadth and tolerance are not indifferentism. Truth *is* many-sided; but truth comes not through the silence of all, but by each declaring earnestly and honestly his best. In no other way can progress in truth be brought about. Each thinker, therefore, recognizes that his own view must be partial, but he puts it forth with all energy and earnestness, for it is the truth for which it is given him to stand. He expects its partial character to be corrected by conflict with the thought of other equally earnest and honest thinkers.

A closely connected danger is that of *making insights or feeling take the place of doing*. The possession of right theories of conduct, carefully thought out, or of kindly emotions, is often assumed to insure right conduct, and as often becomes a snare to their possessor. Knowing the truth is not doing the truth. "Especially," says Stanley Hall, "wherever good precepts are allowed to rest peacefully beside bad discarded habits, moral weakness is directly cultivated."[1] There are temperaments naturally gifted with clear insight and delicately sensitive to the bearings of conduct, who can speak unerringly concerning the temptations, dangers, and aids of living, but whose lives seem none the better. DeQuincy records that this is precisely the state of the opium-eater. Such a character is likely to develop special weakness of will, for there is positive injury in clear insights that are not obeyed; the whole character is cankered by this persistent failure to live according to one's best light, and becomes hollow and hypocritical. *The problem of life cannot be solved on paper*. It is just here that peculiar danger besets those whose business it is to think and speak much along the lines of the moral and the religious life. They easily persuade themselves that having thought and felt and spoken so clearly of the right life, they may rest assured that right conduct will follow as a matter of course. There is danger, at least, that the proverb which Paulsen

[1] *Pedagogical Seminary*, Vol. II, p. 8.

quotes shall prove true: "The man who rings the bell cannot march in the procession."[1]

Among the intellectual hindrances to character, there should be named one special effect of *intellectual vagueness*. It is intellectual vagueness, I believe, which gives the chief danger to many forms of temptation. And the spiritual leader needs to see this both for himself and for others. The temptations are alluring only so long as their real implications are allowed to remain vague in the mind. Let them be fully thought, and their power is gone. They will not bear investigation. They have only the abnormal power of what psychology calls the "insistent ideas" of the insane, that continually impel one to some action that he may even abhor to do.

It is doubtless not advice to be followed in our weaker moods; but sometimes the very best cure for these insistent temptations is no longer to seek simply to evade their thought, but to turn a square look at them. In some clear, high moment of vision, at a time when one is at his best, let him calmly and clearly face the facts as to these

[1] *Cf. A System of Ethics*, pp. 211–214.

things which he has counted his greatest allurements. Let him turn a telescope on the Sirens and the Lorelei — the telescope of a little clear thinking. They are not so attractive as he has thought; their beauty is false and painted; their smile, a leer. It may not be wholly unwise even to take the cotton out of one's ears, and from one's height of vantage to listen for a moment with thoughtful attention to the song of these sirens. A man finds the song coarser than he had thought, and the voices too harsh and too cruel to charm. No! One does not *wish* to let himself go into what are euphemistically called "great passions" of body or mind.

It is a sobering reflection that Lotze gives us, when he says: "We too easily forget that much which looks extremely well in a picture and has a striking effect in poetry, would make us heartily ashamed of our prepossession if we were to see it, not at a single favorable moment but in the ordinary course of life, in connection with all its manifold results. The charm of what is strange and full of characteristic expression and one-sided originality, is so great that it leads every one to be sometimes unjust toward that consistent, thoughtful, steadfast order of civilized life which, though less warm in coloring, is ineffably more worthy."[1] At the "parting of the ways," Lowell promises, if one follows the call of Duty, he shall find her finally more beautiful than Pleasure, and with vastly more to give. The "pilgrim chorus" in Wagner is better music than the "Venus music"; it deserves to drown the other, oneself being judge. Life means more, and love means more, with Elizabeth, than in the "Venus mountain." And definite, clear thinking, avoiding all vagueness, will show it.

Paulsen states the same point with convincing clearness in his *Introduction to Philosophy:* "There is perhaps no man who could look back upon a life full of emptiness and baseness, full of falsehood and cowardice, full of wickedness and depravity, with feelings of satisfaction. At any rate, it would not be advisable for any one to make the trial. The lives of so-called men of the world and their female partners, or of blacklegs and scoundrels, little and big ones, are not apt to be described at length and openly either by themselves or others. Should it

[1] *The Microcosmus,* Vol. II, p. 65.

be done, and perhaps it would not be a useless task, it is not likely that any one would lay aside the book with the feeling: that was a happy and enviable life. And if such a life had achieved an apparent success, if it had committed everything and enjoyed everything with impunity, nevertheless, it would not easily strike an observer as a beautiful and desirable lot."[1]

In the life of the student there are peculiar *dangers in habits of study*. There are situations in life where the power to "cram," for example, is of undoubted value, and its use thoroughly justified, as is not infrequently true in the lawyer's profession in working up technical details required in some particular case. But to rely upon "cramming" in those subjects that make up one's educational course is quite another matter. This is simply to put an easy and sham process in the place of a hard and honest one. This cannot occur without mental and moral loss. A study so pursued cannot have been put in relation to the rest of one's thinking. It is no proper part of the man, and can never become one of his permanent interests. And the habit of merely easy and superficial work

[1] *Op. cit.*, p. 73.

—the baneful want of thoroughness—must have an unfavorable moral effect.

President Stanley Hall calls attention to a similar abuse of elective courses. To use the elective system only as giving opportunity for the choice of easy courses, or of taking many different subjects, is to lose in discipline of both intellect and will. For the beginnings of most subjects are easy; it is only as one pushes on that he can derive from them any severe training.

There is study and study. Much that is so called hardly deserves the name. And the kind of study that a man does affects the whole man. Many students would gain by shortening their hours of so-called study, by stopping more frequently for brief periods of rest, and by studying with determined concentration while at it. This does not mean working on one's nerves, in a tense, strained attitude of mind, but cool, calm, steady attention to the work in hand, and to that alone, even if the mail comes in the midst of one's study. It is a great epoch in a student's career when he has had experience of the joy and achievement of the best concentration of which he is capable. Now he knows what study means, and he cannot again content himself with sitting before an open text-book, while from time to time he recalls his mind from the ends of the earth. Gone are the days of the rocking-chair and the open window, gone are the days of the half-hour's journey to class, and of the fifteen minutes' waiting before lectures, gone are all "gasings" in his precious hours of study— he has learned to study! He has learned how to rest, and he has learned how to play; but he has stopped "fooling around."

II. EMOTIONAL CONDITIONS

Another natural inference from the unity of the mind is that of the influence of feeling on the conduct of life.

The Stimulating Effect of Joyful Emotions. —The observations of physiological psychology show that joyful emotions have a positively stimulating effect, bodily and mental. Henle's researches proved that joyful emotions relax the muscles of the arteries and of the bronchial tubes, quickening the circulation and making respiration freer, and this without the evil consequences which attend anger, though anger, also, relaxes the same muscles. The depressing emotions, on the other hand, like sorrow and fear, contract the arterial and bronchial muscles and so distinctly interfere with both the circulation and breathing. It was long ago observed that blood flowed from an open wound more freely at the sound of music. Recent experiments on hypnotic subjects fully confirm these bodily results of the emotions.

And it is only a broader illustration of the same influence which so careful an observer as Romanes gives, when, writing on the "science and philosophy of recreation," he says: "It is impossible to over-estimate the value of the emotions in this connection — a prolonged flow of happy feeling doing more to brace up the system for work than any other influence operating for a similar length of time."[1] Miss Brackett, consequently, seems justified in saying that there is "no work, whatever it may be, that is so exhausting as painful emotion." "There is no tonic so uplifting and renewing as joy, which sets into active exercise every constructive power of the body."[2]

Whether or not we accept Professor

[1] *Popular Science Monthly*, Vol. XV, pp. 772 ff.
[2] *The Technique of Rest*, p. 117.

James' famous theory of the emotions, that they are simply the feeling of the bodily changes which directly follow the perception of an exciting fact, the observations which make any defense of the theory possible are sufficient evidence that, as he says, "the entire organism may be called a sounding-board, which every change of consciousness, however slight, may make reverberate." "Our whole cubic capacity is sensibly alive, and each morsel of it contributes its pulsation of feeling, dim or sharp, pleasant, painful or dubious, to that sense of personality that every one of us unfailingly carries with him."[1]

Now all these facts not only show again the marvelous intimacy of the relation between mind and body (which is not now the point under consideration), but also help us to see the bearing of emotion on volition, though it is here exerted indirectly through the body; they help us to see why emotion actually increases our sense of reality, and why it must have an important contribution to make to our deepest life.[2] This is peculiarly true of joy, if it is *taken in no shallow*

[1] *Op. cit.*, Vol. II, pp. 450, 451.
[2] *Cf.* King, *Personal and Ideal Elements in Education*, pp. 227 ff.

surface way. It literally makes us live more, and so gives a deeper sense of the reality of all other life. For this very reason it helps directly to convictions which make volition easy. As Keats puts it: "Axioms are not axioms until they have been felt upon our pulses." We are made for joy — body and mind; our very constitution proclaims it. Pain is not a good in itself, and unnecessary depression and needless worry only lessen our power for work, and — what is more — weaken our power to will. The relation is close and simple. Joy directly increases our vitality. Greater vitality gives greater sense of reality. This means stronger convictions. Of convictions purposes are born. And conviction and purpose make influence certain. The spiritual life may not safely ignore these plain facts. Joy has its very distinct mission and place in the spiritual life. Are not Christian ministers too prone to forget that the message they are set to bring is a *gospel*— good news? An ultimate message of hope is essential to the strongest living.

The Danger of Strained and Sham Emotions.— But while real joy has, within limits, a healthful, stimulating influence, strained and sham emotion is to be everywhere avoided, for strained and sham emotion is followed by an inevitable reaction often profound, and by a more dreadful sense of unreality. The hysterical feeling taints with its falseness all else, and so saps conviction and motive for action. "When the soul pretends to graces which are denied it," says Granger, following St. Teresa, "the effect passes quickly, and 'aridity is the result.'"[1] There is a kind of dishonesty, too, involved in these sham emotions that must react unfavorably on the whole life. Moreover, the false emotion hinders the true, and is a positive drain instead of help. Strain is everywhere drain. Neither physically nor mentally are we constituted for continuously tense conditions. And, where the tenseness is forced, we have made impossible normal, wholesome living. Healthful and helpful emotion simply comes as a normal attendant; it is not manufactured.

This counsel against sham and strained emotion has many applications. All personal relations, for example, suffer from hysterical emotion; no true friendship can be built upon a false foundation. And most of the abnormal elements in the religious life may be traced to the same cause. Ritschl seems

[1] *The Soul of the Christian*, p. 127.

quite justified in saying: "The craving after assurance leads to an artificial tension of sentiment, with interruptions by moments of despair, or with the risk of lasting self-deception."[1] "Experiences" of any kind cannot healthfully be sought anywhere as ends in themselves. We shall find this consideration forced upon us later from another point of view, in the need of the objective mood.

The Influence of Moods on Willing.—In considering the emotional conditions of living, one must, also, not forget the great influence of moods on volition. Few great choices are made by a simple, heavy tug of the will. Commonly our moods must favor the will. And here lies the importance of what James has called the "serious and strenuous moods." It is in these moods that it becomes more easily possible for one to see life as it is, more easily possible to do what he ought. These are the natural birth hours of great decisions, and they should not be allowed lightly to pass. The production of the serious and strenuous mood is, moreover, by no means, wholly beyond our power. We can do much to induce the high thoughtfulness that makes us capable of great decisions.

[1] Quoted by Granger, *The Soul of a Christian*, p. 81.

We can, at least, deliberately place ourselves in the presence of the great truths—we can give the spiritual world a chance to make its legitimate impression upon us. On the other hand, one needs so to guard himself that no significant decisions will come into his weak and nerveless moments.

The Danger of Passive Emotion.—Few psychologists from the time of Bishop Butler have failed to notice one other danger connected with the emotions—the danger of merely passive emotion. Höffding quotes Ideler as saying, "Passive emotion only, which is reduced to an empty longing, vain desire, foolish hope, or cowardly denial, is the root of madness."[1] This is strong language, and yet we are all of us, in different degrees, subject to this danger of indulgence in merely passive emotion. It is not the habitué of the theater alone, nor the inveterate novel-reader, who suffers here. By the sure working of mental laws, to indulge merely passive emotion, followed by no action, is just so far to incapacitate ourselves for action. For our capacity for warm feeling under the same circumstances diminishes; and, unless this diminishing emotion is made

[1] *Op. cit.*, p. 338.

good by a habit of action, the time comes when one can not act. These are the facts which lie at the basis of the injunction which every earnest psychologist must urge: Make certain that every right emotion has its prompt and proper expression in action. To be deeply moved to feelings of pity, of sympathy, of aspiration, whether by concert or by sermon, by theater or by novel, and to fail to put this feeling into some form of expression, conduces directly to will-weakening—to a merely passive and sentimental character. The mind is here its own avenger. This consideration needs to be urged in audiences of religious people, for passive religious emotion has identical dangers. The principle, also, indicates the weakness of mere exhortation; the crying need is often for *definite* suggestion or direction of precise ways in which the feeling or resolution stirred may be wisely expressed.

The Need of Power to Withstand Strong Emotion.—Nor should one forget, although it is possible, as I have said, for emotion to add greatly to the sense of reality, that one must often turn from the most exciting emotion and refuse to pass judgment until reason, and not emotion only, bids. The matter must not only seem real; it must also justify itself as *rational* and *ethical*.[1] It has been well said by another that "the highest result of education" is to give the power "to suspend belief in the presence of an emotionally exciting idea."[2] And no man has himself wholly in hand who is without this power. Where reason has already entered its judgment, we may rejoice in all the quickening sense of reality that emotion can give; but where reason holds the decision still in suspense, no emotion can be strong enough to justify belief or to justify action. And, to-day, there are wide-spread tendencies at work which particularly need this "power to suspend belief." As Jastrow says, "the opinions to which we incline are all colored o'er with the deep tinge of emotional reality, which is the living expression of our interest in them or our inclination toward them. What they require is a more vigorous infusion of the pale cast of thought; for the problem of the occult and the temptations to belief which it holds out are such as can be met only by a sturdy application of a critical logic."[3]

[1] *Cf.* King, *Personal and Ideal Elements in Education*, pp. 164 ff.
[2] James, *Psychology*, Vol. II, p. 308.
[3] *Fact and Fable in Psychology*, p. 39.

Nowhere more than in the presence of exciting emotion can a man prove himself worthy of the noble figure of Plato, of the soul as charioteer, driving its four horses abreast and having them all in hand. And to this end, as Höffding says, "we must utilize the intervals between strong emotions." "By bringing ourselves under certain definite conditions, we may further or prevent the birth of certain feelings."[1] But with this consideration we have already entered upon the field of the *volitional* conditions of rational living, which may be best treated in the next great division of our inquiry. Some of the most important suggestions as to emotional conditions, too, it should be borne in mind, will meet us in the later consideration of the fundamental importance of respect for personality.

[1] *Op. cit.*, pp. 334, 333.

THE CENTRAL IMPORTANCE OF WILL AND ACTION

CHAPTER IX

THE CENTRAL IMPORTANCE OF WILL AND ACTION — THE PSYCHOLOGICAL EVIDENCE

"A MAN does what he is at the time," the older psychology said. This the newer psychology reaffirms, but adds with even greater emphasis: a man is at the time what he does. Not feelings, not sentiments, moral sensibilities, or aspirations, not principles, not good resolutions, even, but only action, born of the will, truly reveals us. "If no external action follows upon the internal," asks Höffding, "how can I be certain that I have really willed?" "Many people regard themselves as great heroes of the will, because they have reveled in great resolves, although these never acquired the tangible and prosaic form of external actions." Stanley Hall says: "To live is now to act: acts lay down the primitive strata in the soul, which determine even the deepest belief."[1] This

[1] In article on *Research, the Vital Spirit of Teaching.*

emphasis on action, "the voluntaristic trend" in modern psychology, seems unmistakable; so that Paulsen can say: "Of late, psychology tends more and more to consider will as the primary and constitutive function of the mind."[1] What, then, is the basis of this assertion? What are the psychological facts?

I. THE SUGGESTION OF EVOLUTION

No doubt this "voluntaristic trend" is in part due to the influence of the evolution theory and to the wider view opened up by comparative psychology, which Paulsen has made so prominent in his discussion. If mind is granted to the lower animals, it is difficult to believe that the perceptive function in mind is nearly so fundamental as the active impulsive function. The animal seems to act not so much in view of certain perceptions, as because of certain impulses. Not insight but impulse seems the beginning; and not insight but action seems the end.

II. IMPULSE TO ACTION, FUNDAMENTAL

But if the animal world and the evolutionary origin of man are left quite out of

[1] *Introduction to Philosophy*, p. 113.

account, the psychological importance of action is hardly lessened. Höffding agrees with Paulsen in saying the same thing of man that has been said of the animal. "As Fichte taught," he says, "the most original thing in us is the impulse to action; it is given before the consciousness of the world and cannot be derived from it." Schopenhauer built his philosophy wholly on this conception, deriving "the world as idea" from "the world as will." It is quite in harmony with this when Höffding goes further and says: "Since it has been shown to be the most essential feature of consciousness, that all the individual elements and states are united through one synthetic activity, it may be said that to volitional activity is due the existence of consciousness itself." And he adds later: "But even at the highest stages of mental development, a purpose and a feeling aroused by this purpose, rule the course of thought. The more such a mental center of gravity (the real self) is wanting, the more disconnected will consciousness become." And still further: "And only through firm volition is actual *self-consciousness* possible. What is expressed in the unity and the continuity of memory, and in immediate feeling of self, is completed in the act of will, in which all elements of consciousness coöperate with concentrated force. In our resolves and acts of will, the real unity of our 'self' is most strikingly manifested; in them we learn to know ourselves most clearly and best."[1] It would be hard to make the fundamental character of volitional activity more emphatic.

So Baldwin[2] makes imitative activity the bridge between the earlier and later stages of the development of self-consciousness. Royce, also, points out that there is sometimes "a discontent which prefers even painful experiences to the present pleasures, simply because the painful experiences will give an opportunity for the exertion of those activities which our restless feelings demand." This shows how peculiarly strong the impulse to action often is; and Royce calls attention to the very great biological importance of the phenomenon. He also shows how essential activity is even to perception: "If you are to train the powers of perception, *you must train the conduct of the person who is to learn how to perceive.* Nobody sees more than his activities have prepared him to

[1] *Op. cit.*, pp. 310, 314, 316, 332.
[2] *Mental Development, Methods and Processes*, p. 340.

see in the world."[1] We can hardly fail to see in all this how fundamental the impulse to action is.

III. THE NATURAL TERMINUS OF EVERY EXPERIENCE IS ACTION

But, no doubt, the voluntaristic trend in psychology rests still more obviously upon the fact that the natural terminus of every experience—bodily and mental—is action. In mind and body we are organized for action.

The Body, Organized for Action.— The circulation of the *blood*, we are told, looks to action. "Every act evincing life," says a recent writer on physiology, "is the result of the transformation of potential into kinetic energy, and the object of circulation is to remove waste and provide for such a renewal of tissue and of oxygen as to maintain the normal amount of potential energy within the organism."[2] And a distinguished psychologist says: "The blood has at once both a nourishing and a stimulating effect."[3]

[1] *Op. cit.*, pp. 187, 226.
[2] Health Primers: *The Heart and its Functions*, p. 73.
[3] Höffding, *Outlines of Psychology*, p. 310.

So, too, "the whole *neural organism*," James reminds us, "is, physiologically considered, but a machine for converting stimuli into reactions."[1] It finds its end in action, and the nervous process is never normally complete until it has issued in some form of action. This is what Baldwin calls the law of dynamogenesis, and he regards it as so certain in its operation, that he bases upon it his "dynamogenic method" of child-study, holding that "the infant's hand movements in reaching and grasping are the best index of the kind and intensity of its sensory experiences."[2] That the nervous tissue is such that we become in our bodies readily and certainly bundles of habits, points to the same importance of action. The nervous tissue may well be so made if action is the end.

The *muscular system* tells a similar story. Stanley Hall must be correct in his conclusion that the proportion of muscles in the human anatomy is significant. The human body is made for action, and it has other muscles, as he insists, than those which wag the tongue or move a pen.

President Hall urges especially that "ac-

[1] *Op. cit.*, Vol. II, p. 372.
[2] *Mental Development, Methods and Processes*, p. 44.

tivity is imperatively necessary at adolescence," and that education must provide, at this period, some outlet for activity; that it is even hygienic for the physical to take the lead. The peculiar natural power of all the active instincts at adolescence certainly can never be wisely ignored. At no other time does the human being show so clearly that he is made for action. "The love of excitement and adventure; the fierce combative instinct that delights in danger, in struggle, and even in destruction; the restless ambition that seeks with an insatiable longing to better its position and to climb heights that are yet unscaled; the craving for some enjoyment which not merely gives pleasure but carries with it a thrill of passion,"—all these are particularly in evidence at this period; and it is, surely, as Lecky says, a part of the business of education to find for them a "healthy, useful, or at least harmless sphere of action. In the chemistry of character they may ally themselves with the most heroic as well as with the worst parts of our nature."[1]

But the need of engrossing activity throughout life is hardly less for great numbers of the inadequately trained. A recent

[1] *Op. cit.*, p. 264.

writer voices the complaint of one such character: "'For God's sake,' he began, without preamble, 'can't you, 'mongst all the discoveries you're makin', find something kind o' innocent and excitin' to amuse a man like me?'" "Starved longings," the writer continues, "unrealized desires, overflowing animal spirits without legitimate outlet, unbalanced natures destitute of training in self-control, impoverished aspirations,— these are what lie at the foundation of the social problem which the reformer has to solve, and no remedy which does not take all these into consideration will ever be permanently efficacious."[1] And much of all this goes back at once to the body's need for active expression.

The conclusion of Lotze's careful comparison of the human body with animal bodies is that the human body stands at the head of the scale of creatures, when estimated by capacity for *work*. Some animals are swifter, some are stronger, some are longer-lived, but none has such combined advantages in capacity for work.[2] The human body is made for action.

[1] Martha Baker Dunn, in *Atlantic Monthly*, August, 1904.
[2] *The Microcosmus*, Book IV, Chap. IV.

Now, if the modern psychology is at all justified in its assertion of the unity of man, body and mind, if the relation here is one-half as close as psychology supposes, then these facts about the body of man cannot be without significance for the mind.

The Mind Organized for Action.— And the mind of man does, in truth, furnish a parallel. It, too, in all its experiences, looks to action. The psychologist expresses this by saying that *all consciousness is naturally impulsive;* that is, that every idea tends to pass into action, and would do so if it were not hindered by the presence of other ideas; that exclusive attention to an idea is quite certain, therefore, to bring about the corresponding action, as it were, of itself. The so-called "ideo-motor action" thus, is not to be regarded as exceptional, but rather as the normal type of all action. Cognition thus becomes, as James says, only the cross-section of a current forward toward action. Only hold the end steadily before you, and you will do it.

The sweep of this principle is, usually, hardly recognized. It means that the doing of a thing follows, from simple concentration of attention upon it. It gives new point to the old proverb: "As a man thinketh in his heart, so is he." In both slight and grave matters, the principle seems to hold. Filled with this one idea, we go forward almost as if moved from without, sometimes in a kind of daze, into the performance of the act to which the idea looks. The idea tends of itself to pass into act, and only needs the exclusive field to do so. It is the idea that finds an otherwise vacant mind that gets done; it is the engrossing temptation that conquers. Even the self-regarding desires of the most selfish man, too, Butler long ago pointed out, are necessarily directed outward; they terminate upon things, and call for action.

IV. FOR THE VERY SAKE OF THOUGHT AND FEELING, ONE MUST ACT

It is not only true that thought and feeling tend to pass into action, but that, because of the unity of man, one must act for the very sake of thought and feeling. The "voluntaristic trend" in psychology, therefore, is not, when properly taken, a new one-sidedness, a needed, but extreme and passing fashion of the hour. Certainly it is in no such one-sided way that I mean to defend the principle. That would be to deny the mind's real unity. When psychology insists upon the central importance of action, it is not decrying feeling and thinking; but it is saying that not only do thought and feeling tend to pass into action as their end, but that these cannot themselves come to their highest without some form of expression. Of course the new impression so obtained becomes, again, in its turn, stimulus to further action. Even as to our mental imagery, Royce contends: "The most wholesome training of the imagination is properly to be carried out in connection with the training of conduct."[1]

"Axioms are not axioms until they have been felt upon our pulses," Keats has been quoted as saying. It is still more true to say: Axioms are not axioms until they have been done by our muscles. You will *then* best feel them and best think them. And it holds in even the most abstract realm — in mathematics. This is the chief justification of the great number of comparatively simple problems and original exercises in all our best modern mathematical text-books. The student must repeatedly express his thought, thoroughly to understand or retain it. A

[1] *Op. cit.*, p. 161.

principle applied is a very different thing from a principle held in the abstract. "The idea, the knowledge content, grows out of, as well as leads up to, action," Dewey says. The expression, the application, naturally gives what we call the realizing sense.

The same psychological principle justifies all laboratory and seminar methods. There is no other justification of the large amount of time given to working out in the laboratory, principles and statements that could be learned in themselves in a fraction of the time given. It is justly believed that only as the statements and principles are worked out by the student himself, can they be grasped with full intelligence. One must do, to know. What Kedney says of the artist is true of every man: His idea or ideal "is not his till he has expressed it, and is more completely his the more perfect the expression." "A thing known," says Fremantle, "is a thing incorporated into the human personality and made spiritual."[1]

Wundt's deeply significant principle of the "*heterogony of ends*," suggests how far-reaching in its effects expressive activity may be. "We

---

[1] Kedney's *Hegel's Aesthetics*, p. 111; *The World, the Subject of Redemption*, p. 30.

mean to express by this name," he says, "what is a matter of universal experience: that manifestations of will, over the whole range of man's free voluntary actions, are always of such a character that the effects of the actions extend more or less widely beyond the original motives of volition, so that *new* motives are originated for future actions, and again, in their turn, produce new effects." "Its essential warrant is this: that owing to the constant influence of accessory factors the result of every act of choice is as a whole not congruent with the end ideated in the motive. But those elements of the result that lie outside of the original motive are eminently fitted to become new motives, or elements in new motives, from which new ends or variations of the original end arise."[1] Wundt believes this principle to be one of the most important laws in all moral development, and it certainly puts in new light the supreme importance of expressive activity. For it means not merely that the bare thought which we now have demands expression; but that many *new* relations of our thought will never come out

[1] *Ethics: The Facts of the Moral Life*, Eng. Tr., p. 330; *Cf.* pp. 208, 226, 243–247.

for us until we have expressed it. Not only the *reality* of our present thinking, consequently, but our *growth*, intellectual and moral, demands expressive activity. Through active expression we come into an increasingly rich and complex life.

It is even true, as Höffding says, that "the development of the will *in general* reacts upon the *thought*, strengthening and modifying it. A firm resolve, carried out with decision and without hesitation, clears up the whole mental atmosphere and scatters the clouds which dim the clearness of thought; it makes one single idea the central point of consciousness, and obliges all other ideas to give way before this one, or to subordinate themselves to it. Hence arises a firm and systematic connection of consciousness. Sequence of thought and firmness of character are closely related."[1]

To attain, then, any real unity of the whole man, one must act. It was Carlyle's recognition of Goethe's "religion of the deed," not of feeling, Seeley thinks, that led him so vigorously to urge upon his generation: "Close thy Byron; open thy Goethe." Not ideal emotion, but ideal action is the aim.

---

[1] *Op. cit.*, p. 331; *Cf.* also Baldwin, *Mental Development, Methods and Processes*, p. 361.

V. THE WILL IN ATTENTION

The will reveals itself most directly in *attention*. It is often said sweepingly that a man's environment makes him. Not to insist upon the obvious fact that there must be a germ with a certain nature in order that any environment may work its effect, it is particularly important to notice in the case of man, that not his *entire* environment, but only that part of his environment to which he *attends* really makes him. "The fundamental truth is," as Hoffman says, "that interest is primarily the product of attention, not the reverse."[1] The same world, as we have seen, is a very different world to different men. Even advancing civilization is no guaranty of each individual's ethical progress. As Wundt says: "The ethical influence of civilization is everywhere ambiguous. As it helps to deepen and refine men's moral ideas, so it opens up all sorts of paths which may lead him from the good." "The only legitimate enquiry is, what *means* civilization places at the disposal of the will that has decided to follow the good."[2]

[1] *Psychology and Common Life*, p. 41.
[2] *The Facts of the Moral Life*, pp. 322, 324.

Here — in attention — the believer in the freedom of the will will not doubt, lies the precise sphere of that freedom. One can choose to what he will attend. And it is the idea to which he attends that passes into *action*. One's environment, thus, need not make him; he may make his environment, as every man of masterly will shows. Such wills are not made by environment. It is time that we reasserted with all our might Kant's old doctrine that we *can*, if we ought. The prevalent determinism in theory (though it arises from a false "psychologism," as Münsterberg calls it),[1] is likely balefully to affect practical action.[2] We *may* overdo in our social plans the modern emphasis on environment, important as that is. In a very real sense, let us be sure, every one of us makes his own world. "Every man," Smiles says, "stamps his own value upon himself, and we are great or little according to our will." One's sole responsibility is to attend, to concentrate attention on those considerations and ends that ought to prevail; then they will prevail and pass into act. We need not be puppets.

[1] *Psychology and Life*, pp. 20 ff., especially p. 23.
[2] *Cf.* James, *Psychology*, Vol. II, pp. 574–576.

Such attention, moreover, lies at the basis of self-control, and self-control is the chief differentiation of men from animals, of the sane from the insane, and a root-principle of all virtues. The animal, as James says, has a "hair-trigger constitution," and action follows impulse at once; the man may deliberate, and, keeping his attention fixed on some future good, hold the present impulse in check. The insane, too, let themselves go; the sane can prove their complete sanity only by keeping themselves in hand, once more, through the direction of attention. It is obvious, also, that without such self-control no virtue, not even the lowest prudence, is possible. Here, again, there must always be the subordination of present impulse to future good. The will, then, in that power of attention which gives self-control, is absolutely vital.

VI. THE PREËMINENT INFLUENCE OF PRACTICAL INTERESTS IN ALL CONSCIOUSNESS[1]

But it is the preëminent influence of practical interests in all consciousness that testifies most strongly to the central importance of

[1] *Cf.* Bowne, *Theory of Thought and Knowledge*, pp. 370 ff.

action. Many a man not a psychologist can confirm Professor Barnes' observation that a child's first question about a thing is, What is it for? Why? That is, the child's interest is practical and looks at once to action. Professor James has brought out this immense influence of the practical interests with special force, and it is one of his most significant contributions to psychology. It underlies many of the strongest passages in his larger work on psychology, and is the germ of much of his later writing.

In Conceiving and Naming Things.— Practical interests largely determine our modes of conceiving and naming things. "The essence of a thing," our author says, "is that one of its properties which is so *important for my interests* that in comparison with it I may neglect the rest." "But the essence, the ground of conception, varies with the end we have in view." Oil, for example, "one man conceives as a combustible, another as a lubricator, another as a food; the chemist thinks of it as a hydro-carbon; the furniture-maker as a darkener of wood," etc. That is, "*The only meaning of essence is teleological* [looking to ends in action], *and classification and conception are purely teleological weapons of the mind*"; that is, they have their significance as means to ends set in action. "*There is no property* ABSOLUTELY *essential to any one thing.*" In all this conceiving and naming of things, then, it is plain, practical interests — the needs of some course of conduct — are exerting virtually decisive weight.[1]

In Reasoning.— This influence of our interests in the picking out of qualities in a thing is our main dependence in reasoning also. The exceptional reasoner is the man who discerns exactly the right property in a thing, the precise element in the circumstances, which is important for the purpose in hand; and this property or element is much more likely to be discovered by one who not only has *numerous* interests that will lead him to look at the thing from many points of view, but whose present immediate *practical* interest tends to direct his attention to the precise property or element now required for his aim.

In Our Philosophical Solutions.— Even our ultimate philosophical solutions must be, probably, prevailingly practical.

The great influence of practical interests in conception and reasoning implies this.

[1] *Op. cit.*, Vol. II, pp. 335, 333.

The teleological nature of these processes carries important applications in some of the most difficult problems of philosophy, both in metaphysics and in theory of knowledge. In metaphysics it would seem to mean that the only possible ultimate definition of the essence of a thing must be in terms of the purpose of the Infinite—what God meant it to be—the part he meant it to play in the world. In other words, our ultimate metaphysical conceptions must be expressed in volitional or practical terms, in terms of action. This requires a teleological view of the universe.

It is a precisely similar application of this principle which Dewey makes in the sphere of the theory of knowledge: "The unsatisfactory character," he says, "of the entire neo-Kantian movement is in its assumption that knowledge gives birth to itself, and is capable of affording its own justification. The solution . . . reveals itself when we conceive of knowledge as a statement of action, that statement being necessary, moreover, to the successful on-going of action."[1] We know to live, not live to know.

And, after all, if *we* are made for action,

[1] *The Signification of the Problem of Knowledge*, p. 17.

in body and in mind; if *we* are prevailingly practical, it need not seem so strange that our philosophy, too, must depend mainly on practical considerations. We carry our only possible standard of reality within us. To a being for whom no process, physical or mental, is normally complete until it terminates in action, full philosophical convictions can hardly be possible apart from their bearing on conduct.

Moreover, if we are made for action, it is fitting enough that those convictions which are to give support to action should be wrought out in action. The principle of the laboratory method would, in some way, be here preëminently justified. If even abstract truths need to be expressed to be appreciated, still more must those ultimate convictions that underlie all our life.

In truth, when one thinks deeply enough about it, he must see, further, that for the most fundamental problems no other than a practical solution is possible in the nature of the case. There can be no mere theoretical proof or disproof of the trustworthiness of our faculties, for example,—a problem about which Pascal tormented himself. One could only use the very faculties in question in such a proof. The only proof possible is the practical power to use them. So, too, one can prove the world a sphere of rational thought and rational action only by *using his powers* in it. And yet these convictions underlie every possible thought and action, and we reassert them in every moment of our life. If we chose to deny them, we should have to do so by virtue of reasoning that assumed their validity; for the denial involves the assumption that we can think—that things are thinkable.

Into the very fiber of certain of our most indubitable convictions, even,—our so-called innate judgments—something of the practical, Lotze believes, is wrought.[1] And he ends his latest book on metaphysics with the assertion of his first book, that ethics must determine metaphysics; the *ought* must determine the *is* and the *must*. It is interesting to find Paulsen and Wundt agreeing in this insistence of Lotze's. Paulsen says that morality may "serve as a starting-point and support for metaphysics. And this is precisely what I believe."[2] Wundt says distinctly: "I think that we must look to ethics to supply the corner-

[1] *The Microcosmus*, Vol. I, p. 671.
[2] *A System of Ethics*, Eng. Tr., p. 448.

stones of metaphysics, of our final and comprehensive view of the universe."[1] And in this emphasis these later thinkers are following directly in the footsteps of Kant and Fichte.

There is a moral tonic in the very atmosphere of these men — Kant with his tremendous emphasis on the "practical reason"—on will; Fichte with his constant sense of "vocation." Paulsen himself says of Kant: "The worth of a man depends on his *will*, not on his *knowledge* . . . ; — that is the cardinal doctrine upon which Kant's entire philosophy really turns."[2] "In one word," says Fichte, "it is only by thorough amelioration of the will that a new light is thrown on our existence and future destiny; without this let me meditate as much as I will, and be endowed with ever such rare intellectual gifts, darkness remains within me and around me." "I know immediately what is necessary for me to know, and this will I joyfully and without hesitation or sophistication practice." This message of Fichte, Carlyle, in his own way, catches up in the familiar words of his *Sartor Resartus:* "Doubt of any kind cannot

[1] *The Facts of the Moral Life*, p. VI.
[2] *A System of Ethics*, Eng. Tr., p. 200.

be removed, except by action. On which ground, too, let him who gropes painfully in darkness or uncertain light, and prays vehemently that dawn may ripen into day, lay this other precept well to heart—Do the duty which lies nearest thee."

We may hope that the real ground of this counsel is becoming increasingly clear to our later thinking; but it was never mere shallow advice to forget one's questions in doing. The ethical attitude and action were felt to be necessary to reach the point of view whence a solution was possible. The significance of the situation opened itself only so. Action brought experience of some new value that we could not choose before with full heart, because we did not know it. New ends, as we have found Wundt suggesting, have arisen for us.

Our own generation, we have seen, is inclined to add that the ultimate problems are, in the nature of the case, such as to make a purely theoretical solution impossible. So James says: "If we survey the field of history and ask what feature all great periods of revival, of expansion of the human mind, display in common, we shall find, I think, simply this: that each and all of them have said to the human being, 'The inmost nature of the reality is congenial to *powers* which you possess.'" "In a word, 'Son of man, *stand upon thy feet* and I will speak unto thee!' is the only revelation of truth to which the solving epochs have helped the disciple. But that has been enough to satisfy the greater part of his rational need."[1]

Since doubt is never a reason for action, this willingness to use one's powers implies faith, and so this passage of James becomes practically parallel to one from Goethe: "The deepest, nay, the only theme of the world's history is the conflict of faith and unbelief. The epochs in which faith, in whatever form it may be, prevails, are the marked epochs in human history, full of heart-stirring memories and of substantial gain for all after times."[2]

It is noteworthy that the two books of the Bible that alone may be called philosophical— Job and Ecclesiastes — give, also, only a practical solution. Job's problem gets no complete theoretical solution, though light is thrown upon it; only in the completer revelation of what God is, he gets patience to wait. His vision of the majesty of God

---

[1] *Psychology*, Vol. II, pp. 314, 315.
[2] Quoted by Lecky, *Op. cit.*, p. 229.

gives faith in a solution which as yet he cannot see. And that other curiously modern book—that of "the debater concerning life's meaning" and value, Ecclesiastes—has only to say at the end, after all attempted and partial solutions, and in a kind of protest against any merely theoretical solvent: "And furthermore, my son, be admonished; of making many books there is no end; and much study is a weariness of the flesh. This is the end of the matter; all hath been heard; fear God and keep his commandments; for this is the whole of man."[1] Only the right life could satisfy.

I was interested to notice how often, among Christian university students in Berlin, the practical solution was chosen, in the emphasis on Christ's words: "If any man willeth to do his will, he shall know of the teaching, whether it be of God, or whether I speak from myself." Christianity is no ready-made and all-inclusive answer to curious questions, but brings only that fundamental assurance that suffices for faith and work. But the spirit which Christianity so calls forth is the very spirit in which one will most surely find the world a rational world by using his powers in it.

[1] Ecclesiastes, 12:12, 13.

VII. SOME CURRENT PSYCHOLOGICAL EMPHASES

Not only the express testimony of psychologists, but current phenomena in psychological literature bear witness to this "voluntaristic trend." James' vigorous complaint of the neglect by the English empiricist school of "the perpetual presence of selective attention," and his own constant emphasis on it, evince a strong sense of the active elements in consciousness.[1] Baldwin's like complaint of the "extraordinary neglect" by psychologists of the topic of imitation, and the fundamental and continuous place, which he, as well as Professor Royce, give to imitative activity in all development, both of the individual and of society, show the same trend. Both volumes of Baldwin's *Mental Development* may be said, indeed, to be almost devoted to the proof of the importance of "conscious imitation." Now, whether Baldwin's precise formulation of his thesis be accepted or not, the phenomena to which he appeals in proof do show the tremendous importance of volitional activity. In quite another way, Dr. Harris' constant use, in his *Psychological Foundations of Education*, of the principle

[1] *Psychology*, Vol. I, p. 402.

of self-activity as the ultimate principle in the treatment of the mind, is a similar emphasis. And no one has given a broader application of the need of intelligently directed action in education than Professor Dewey in his *The School and Society*.

Many other names might be added to the list, but perhaps no one has more strongly or clearly emphasized the central importance of the will than Professor Münsterberg in his recent book on *Psychology and Life*, in which, in close sympathy with Fichte, man's *whole life is defined in terms of the will*. The range of his thought requires a long quotation, and may serve, also, as a kind of summary of the preceding discussion. "Far from allowing psychology," he says, "to doubt whether the real life has duties, we must understand that there is no psychology, no science, no thought, no doubt, which does not, by its very appearance, solemnly acknowledge that it is the child of duties. Psychology may dissolve our will and our personality and our freedom, and it is constrained by duty to do so, but it must not forget that it speaks only of that will and that personality which are by metamorphosis substituted for the personality and the will of real life, and that it is this real personality and its free will which create psychology in the service of its ends and aims and ideals."

"In the real life we are willing subjects whose reality is given in our will attitudes, in our liking and disliking, loving and hating, affirming and denying, agreeing and fighting; and, as these attitudes overlap and bind one another, this willing personality has unity. We know ourselves by feeling ourselves as those willing subjects; we do not perceive that will in ourselves; we will it." "History speaks only of those will acts which are acknowledged as merely individual. We know other will acts in ourselves which we will with an over-individual meaning, those attitudes we take when we feel ourselves beyond the domain of our purely personal wishes." "If the system of our individual will acts is interpreted and connected in the historical sciences, the system of our over-individual will acts is interpreted and connected in the normative sciences, logic, æsthetics, ethics, and philosophy of religion. Logic treats of the over-individual will acts of affirming the world, æsthetics, of those of appreciating the world, religion, of those of transcending the world, ethics, of those of acting for the world." "On the basis of these normative sciences, the idealistic philosophy has to build up its metaphysical system which may connect the disconnected will attitudes of our ethical, æsthetical, religious and logical duties in one ideal dome of thoughts."[1] "The world we will," thus Professor Münsterberg says, "is the reality; the world we perceive is the deduced, and therefore unreal system."

Professor Dewey's fundamental principle "that society, whether from the side of association (sociology) or of individualization (psychology), is to be interpreted with reference to active interests or organized interactions, not with reference to thoughts, intellectual contents," shows at least a closely related view. Now the very possibility of such a definition of life in terms of will, whether one wholly accepts it or not, is an impressive proof of the central importance of will.

The facts which have been passed in review give ample ground for the "voluntaristic trend" in psychology, and for belief in the central importance of will and action: —impulse to action the deepest thing in us; every experience, bodily and mental, tending to terminate in action; expression required for the sake of thought and feeling; the

[1] *Psychology and Life*, pp. 23–28. (Abridged.)

decisive power of the will in attention; the predominant influence of practical interests in consciousness; the fact that even our philosophical solutions are prevailingly practical; current phenomena in psychological literature; and especially the possibility of defining the whole of man's life in terms of will. Matthew Arnold might well say that conduct was three-fourths of life.

Hence we may not hope to come to clear and comprehensive views of the rational management of life without careful recognition of these facts now passed in review,—of the importance of will and action. Manifestly, these facts touch upon our character, our happiness, our influence, at every point. What definite suggestions, now, for rational and ethical and spiritual living has this third great insistence of modern psychology? Many practical inferences have been already implied in setting forth the psychological facts; but there are certain counsels which deserve more precise statement.

CHAPTER X

*THE CENTRAL IMPORTANCE OF WILL AND ACTION—
SUGGESTIONS FOR LIVING*

I. THE ENORMOUS PLACE OF WILL AND ACTION IN LIFE

IN the first place, these facts give a new sense of the enormous place of will in life, and of the need of definite will-training. "If," says that psychologist who has done more than any other to make psychology vital, "the 'searching of our heart and reins' be the purpose of this human drama, then what is sought seems to be what effort we can make. He who can make none is but a shadow; he who can make much is a hero." "And the effort which he is able to put forth to hold himself erect and keep his heart unshaken is the direct measure of his worth and function in the game of human life."[1] Life has its reality, its meaning, its interest, its end, in the will-attitudes which we take. We have already seen how Münster-

[1] James, *Psychology*, Vol. II, p. 578.

berg urges the prime significance of the will-attitudes. We cannot ignore this if we care to count at all. We must will, not merely think or feel. Even the "ills of life," Martineau reminds us, "are not here on their own account, but are as a divine challenge and God-like wrestling in the night with our too reluctant wills." Life fails of its purpose for us, if it does not call out the heroic will.

The training of will becomes, thus, the most vital of all problems. "But the education of the will," Lecky believes,—"the power of breasting the current of the desires, and doing for long periods what is distasteful and painful—is much less cultivated than in some periods of the past." If Lecky's judgment is correct here, the fact is, nevertheless, quite inconsistent with the present psychological emphasis, and most unfortunate as well; for, as Lecky himself says, "nothing which is learned in youth is so really valuable as the power and the habit of self-restraint, of self-sacrifice, of energetic, continuous and concentrated effort."[1]

And strength of will bears not only upon character, but upon happiness and influence

[1] *Op. cit.*, pp. 246, 251.

as well. Will-weakening indulgences, therefore, sap the worth of life at all points. That strength of will bears upon *character*, needs no argument. Character lies preëminently in the sphere of the will; he who would achieve much in the moral life must be capable of mighty purposes and mighty endeavors. The place of will in *influence* is hardly less obvious. Only he who can set his goal and steadily and firmly pursue it can hope to count greatly with others.

A large part, even of our own *happiness*, is to be found in just this vigorous exercise of our wills. Practically all our sports and games, it is worth noting, are simply devices for setting up obstacles for the fun of getting over them. "Play is the child of work," Wundt says. We are made for action, and we cannot be even happy in constant inactivity.[1] It is an interesting testimony that Walter Wellman bears concerning his journey toward the north pole, with the thermometer from forty to forty-eight degrees below zero: "It was glorious thus to feel one's strength, to fear nothing in the way of hardship or exertion, to carry a consciousness of superiority to all the obstacles which nature has

[1] *Cf.* Paulsen, *System of Ethics*, pp. 258 ff.

placed in our path. I was never happier than in these hard days."

Lotze shows, in a thoughtful passage, how surely this powerful putting forth of the will in struggle and wide endeavor contributes to the highest happiness: "By the opposition which the natural course of things offers to a too easy satisfaction of natural impulses; by the labor to which man is compelled, and in the prosecution of which he acquires knowledge of, and power over, things in the most various relations; finally, by misfortune itself and the manifold painful efforts which he has to make under the pressure of the gradually multiplying relations of life: by all this there is both opened before him a wider horizon of varied enjoyment, and also there becomes clear to him, for the first time, the inexhaustible significance of moral Ideas which seem to receive an accession of intrinsic worth with every new relation to which their regulating and organizing influence is extended."[1] Wundt distinctly contrasts man with the animals in two respects, both of which mean strong emphasis on action. "In the case of man, on the other hand, there are two principal factors at work to make

[1] *The Microcosmus*, Vol. II, p. 78.

both individual and social life immeasurably richer and more complex. The one is to be found in the free exercise of *will;* the other in that comprehensive *prevision*, that consideration of past and future in their bearings upon the present, of which man alone is capable."[1]

II. THE FUNDAMENTAL CHARACTER OF SELF-CONTROL

This emphasis on will and action means, moreover, emphasis on self-control as a prime condition of character and of happiness and of influence. If will has, in truth, anything like the place our discussion has indicated, if self-control is the chief differentiation of the human and sane life from the animal and insane life, and a root-principle of all virtues, then the positive conditions of self-control are at the same time primary elements in the right, the happy, and the influential life.

Self-control Fundamental to a Moral and Religious Character.—That self-control is fundamental to character, few probably would deny. It may not be without value, however, to point out that the same condition holds

[1] *Op. cit.*, p. 131.

for the religious life. The hysterical everywhere—most of all, we may be sure, in the religious life—is fundamentally at fault, though, curiously enough, it is here often not only excused but even urged as a particularly high attainment. We may be sure such reasoning is seriously astray, though the mistake arises naturally enough. It substitutes a heathen idea of inspiration for the Christian—a being swept away out of our faculties for that high and complete surrender of ourselves to God in which, in truth, self-control is highest and most completely positive. No attitude is ethical, and therefore religious, into which the will does not positively enter, in which the man does not have himself in hand; and this remains true however religious a man may believe his ecstacy to be. Many sad blots in the history of religion would have been impossible, if men had kept this principle clearly in mind. In this sense, President Jordan's protest against "revivals in which men lose their reason and self-control," was wholly justified. A genuine revival of religion is a revival of the highest reason and the most strenuous self-control (though with strong emotion), and that not merely as restraints but as positive motives.

Self-control Fundamental to Happiness.—It is, perhaps, still less obvious that self-control is fundamental to happiness, though this I believe to be equally true. For unless one is prepared to assert outright that the completest happiness for man lies in a going back to the animal, and in a cultivation of insanity, he can hardly doubt that self-control is necessary to the completest happiness, even on the lower plane of the appetites and passions. It is worthy of note that Aristippus, the Cyrenaic, the avowed sum of whose philosophy was to extract the utmost of pleasure out of each passing moment, was true enough, not only to his Socratic teaching, but to the facts, to affirm that this getting the utmost pleasure required, at the very moment of its tasting, a self-mastery. "I hold," he said, "I am not held;" that is, I master my pleasures; my pleasures do not master me.[1] This principle of Aristippus seems to me to be a piece of accurate psychological observation. We are so made that we cannot get the most and best, even upon the lowest planes, without keeping ourselves in hand, without a permeating element of self-mastery; we cannot simply let ourselves go.

[1] *Cf.* Zeller, *Socrates and the Socratic Schools*, pp. 366, 361, 367.

And this self-mastery must not be a mere restraint, holding ourselves back; it must be a positive and definite making the lower serve the higher. Nor can it be counterfeited for the mere sake of the greater pleasure; the right attitude must be there, to taste the pleasure's full sweetness. The pathway to the largest happiness is that of true modesty, which lies, as one of our philosophers has said, neither in disparagement of nature, nor in exaltation of nature, whether as impassioned voluptuousness or as coarse realism, but in a middle path of real delicacy of feeling which shows a self-control born of a deep sense of the worth of personality and the individual soul.

We are not satisfied that eating, for example, should be "merely a matter of appeasing appetite." The half sense of shame with which one on a railway train takes down his lunch-box and proceeds to devour its contents alone, bears witness to something more than mere lack of companionship. Such eating, it half seems to us, ought to be done behind the door as a necessary, indeed, but rather unseemly process. We do not believe that "ugly and soulless eagerness" in eating and drinking bring the fullest enjoyment of even those processes themselves. We crave the æsthetic accompaniments of the ordered meal, or the social delights of the companionship of others, or some other evidence of the presence of the higher, not merely as added elements of pleasure, but as necessary, that even the eating and drinking themselves may be most enjoyed. The æsthetic may be so violated as not simply to offend our taste but as positively to take away all appetite. The lower must serve the higher. Man is a unity; he cannot deny this unity in any part and not suffer even in that part; he must somehow learn to spiritualize the physical even for the sake of the physical. "Hence," Herrmann can say, "the very sternness of duty which hurts the feelings of the natural man, becomes to the Christian a promise of *hidden* riches, which await him in endless profusion."

Browning's ideal is a true one:

> " Let us not always say,
>   ' Spite of this flesh to-day
> I strove, made head, gained ground upon the whole.'
>   As the bird wings and sings,
>   Let us cry, ' All good things
> Are ours, nor soul helps flesh more, now, than flesh
>   helps soul!'"

There is, indeed, a *temporary sense of power* and a kind of mad ecstasy, as Hawthorne has noted, in the absence of all scruple, in throwing to the winds all self-control. "For guilt," he says, "has its moment of rapture, too. The foremost result of a broken law is ever an ecstatic sense of freedom. And thus [for Miriam and Donatello] there exhaled upward (out of their dark sympathy, at the base of which lay a human corpse) a bliss, or an insanity, which the unhappy pair imagined to be well worth the sleepy innocence that was forever lost to them. . . . Forevermore cemented with his blood." It was this power of insanity, this ecstasy of overleaping all bounds, that Schlegel mistook for reality and tried to make the basis of a philosophy for the Romanticists in his "standpoint of irony"; but it is only the power and the joy of madness, none the less. It is the power and the joy which a man has when all self-control is gone. Self-control, then, we may believe, in the positive sense of a subordination of the lower to the higher, is necessary to happiness as well as to character.

Self-Control Fundamental to Influence.—Positive self-control is as necessary to the highest influence as to character and happiness. A man gives small promise of mastery of other forces and other men who has not mastered himself. The leader must show *reserved power*, must make it plain that he has himself in hand, if he is to secure confidence. Lack of self-control reveals itself in subtle ways, and nothing snaps so surely the tie of sympathy and faith between leader and led. This is true even where, from a mistaken point of view, the lack of self-control is excused or even justified and gloried in by a man's followers. Even against their will their confidence is broken. To no leader of men is the highest and finest self-control so vital as to the religious leader. He denies his very calling when he fails here. He may well covet the keenest perception at this point. The fag and strain which hinder any leadership are well nigh fatal for him. There must be no hint or suspicion of the strained and the hysterical in him or in his speaking, if he wishes to count to his utmost. Religion, let us be sure that men see, is life — the broadest, largest, deepest, richest life. Bathed in it, permeated with it, we are to speak out of it with an enthusiasm and joy that need no exaggeration and allow no belittling.

Self-Control Positive, not Negative.— Remembering that the great battlefield of the will is in attention, and that the chief physical condition of attention is surplus nervous energy; and keeping in mind the general intellectual and emotional helps and hindrances to normal will-action already discussed, it is worth while, here, to emphasize the fact already mentioned, that self-control —in spite of its name—to be most effective must be positive, not negative.

As to control of emotions, it may be said at once that we have to depend chiefly on an indirect control of feeling through either attention or action. Over feeling itself we have no direct power; it arises involuntarily in the presence of its exciting object; but we *can* determine to what objects we will attend. We can thus train our thinking through the will in attention, and our thinking finally determines our feeling. So, too, we can act in the line of the feelings we would have, and the reflex effect of the persistent action on the emotion can be quite surely counted on. The mien and attitude and action of cheerfulness and courage will go far in producing the mood of cheer and courage.

But these methods of control of emotion

by attention in thinking and by action are positive, as they ought to be; for, as Höffding says, "let it not be forgotten that self-control, considered as a negative virtue, is a psychological impossibility. It is too often left out of sight in ethics that one impulse can only be displaced by another."[1] So Royce says still more broadly: "The rule of inhibition as regards the before-mentioned hierarchy of the nervous centers, seems to be that *the higher a given function is, the more numerous are the inhibitory influences that it exercises over lower centers.*" "Whenever we can get higher functions of a positive sort established, we thereby train inhibitory tendencies." "*You teach a man to control or restrain himself as soon as you teach him what to do in a positive sense.* Healthy activity includes self-restraint, or inhibition, as one of its elements. *You in vain teach, then, self-control, unless you teach much more than self-control.*" This is the reason for one of the great weaknesses, it may be noticed in passing, of much preaching and moral instruction — it is mere exhortation, giving no direct suggestion of positive achievement. Royce adds, sugges-

[1] *The Law of Relativity in Ethics, International Journal of Ethics*, Vol. I, pp. 30 ff.

tively, of the danger of mere negative inhibition: "In persons of morbidly conscientious life, such inhibitory phenomena may easily get an inconvenient, and sometimes do get a dangerous intensity. The result is, then, a fearful, cowardly, helpless attitude toward life—an attitude which defeats its own aim and renders the sufferer not, as he intends to be, 'good,' but a positive nuisance."[1]

The true psychological method, therefore, is always positive, not merely negatively fighting a thought, trying to withhold attention from it (which only holds it the more certainly in mind), but positively turning the attention to some other thought—not refusing to attend to this, but positively attending to something else. The law is very simple. One cannot get an empty mind, and, on the other hand, one cannot think with concentrated attention of two thoughts at the same time. This is the principle of expelling the evil by the good, that so fills the New Testament. "Humanity," as *Ecce Homo* discerns, "changed from a restraint to a motive"—"the enthusiasm for humanity." It is the "thou shalt" set over against the "thou shalt not." And Spinoza only caught up Paul's

[1] *Op. cit.*, pp. 74, 76, 77.

principle of Christian liberty, as he lays it down for the Galatians, when he wrote, as Professor James phrases him: "Anything that a man can avoid under the notion that it is bad, he may also avoid under the notion that something else is good. He who habitually acts under the negative notion, the notion of the bad, is called a slave by Spinoza. To him who acts habitually under the notion of good, he gives the name of freeman." We are to aspire to the good as the best possible way of fighting evil. It is the business of the spiritual leader to make Christian freemen.

No modern statement of this principle has approached in extent of influence and in practical effectiveness Dr. Chalmers' sermon on "The Expulsive Power of a New Affection." Its felicitous title has become a commonplace among preachers; but its central thought deserves such attention and emphasis as it has seldom yet received. It means, put positives for negatives; don't "don't"; covet earnestly the best gifts. Making self-control positive involves, then, *two things:* (1) keeping the attention fixed on the goods, the higher considerations, the future better things that ought to prevail; and (2) thereby everywhere making the lower serve the higher. The problem of character becomes, thus, ultimately a problem of *fixing attention*.

What, now, are the conditions of keeping attention fixed on any thought? Voluntary attention to an absolutely identical object, it should be realized, is possible even for an adult for but the briefest time.

The object *must continually change* for us, if it is to hold attention. The secret of fixing attention on an object, therefore, lies in discerning its different aspects and relations. That a thought may keep its power with us, it must be frequently re-shaped, thought again in new form and new relations and new applications. There must be no unthought phrases. This power of discerning manifold aspects and relations of a thing goes back again to the *possession of a large circle of interests*, and gives a fundamental reason why any high leader of men should be a man of the broadest training and interests. If he is to hold the attention of others to high themes and great causes, he must be able to present them freshly from many points of view, in varied aspects, with multiplied application and illustration. The problem of self-control, of all righteousness, and of all spiritual influence, therefore, is not that of a mere heavy tug of the will. Self-control depends on attention, and attention has its chief support in strong and many-sided interest. This means that the great secret of all living is the *persistent staying in the presence of the best* — the great facts, the great truths, the great personalities, the one great Person, Christ. We come into the absorbing, passionate, and deepening interest in all things of value only so, and it is this persistent, passionate interest in the best that determines, ultimately, our significance and efficiency in life.

III. OBJECTIVITY A PRIME CONDITION OF CHARACTER, AND HAPPINESS, AND INFLUENCE

This brings us at once to a third great practical inference from psychology's emphasis on will and action. If we are made for action, and no experience is normally completed until it issues in action, then the normal mood, it would seem, must be the mood of activity, of work, not of passivity, of brooding — objectivity, not subjectivity or introspection.

No Activity Is at Its Best When the Attention Is Centered on the Self.—One must lose himself in the object. Many illustrations will occur to one. One will best hit the mark when he is thinking of *it*, not of how he is performing the action. The fundamental condition in art-appreciation, Schopenhauer insists, is that one lose himself in the art-object. One of the most interesting things at the Dresden Gallery, after seeing Raphael's great picture of the Sistine Madonna oneself, is watching others see it. It is so evident that practically all come to the picture, saying to themselves: "This is one of the greatest pictures in the world; am I now having the appropriate emotions in the presence of this great picture?" And so long as one is wondering if he is having the appropriate emotions, the picture itself gets no fair chance at one. So, too, one can never be at his best in the company of those with whom he feels himself still on probation. Only those friends see one's best with whom one can quite forget himself in his theme. Health, itself, suffers when one thinks too much about it. Health, rather, requires something of interest to which one can turn and forget himself. One may, perhaps, sum up this need of the objective mood in the immortal rhyme that Mrs. Wiggin has made familiar to us:

> "The centipede was happy quite,
>   Until the frog for fun,
>   Said 'Pray, which leg comes after which?'
>   Which wrought his mind to such a pitch,
>   He lay distracted in a ditch,
>   Considering *how* to run."

It is true of the two best things in the world—*happiness and character*—for the very reason that both are conditions of the self, that they are best found by not seeking them directly. And Bradley's sneer—sharp as it is—at John Stuart Mill for holding to a *summum bonum* that could only be hit by not aiming at it, was itself beside the mark. How often our elaborate preparations for a good time quite fail; and how often, on the other hand, our good time comes on us unawares; but when we study its conditions and think we have discovered its secret, the repetition soon undeceives us. Both the inveterate pleasure-seeker, and many of those most in earnest for character have made the same mistake here—they concentrate their attention too much upon themselves. Both character and happiness require objectivity.

There are two contrasted theories of growth in character, it has been pointed out—one, "the realism of self-development"—the other, "the idealism of work." The one looks at everything to discover its bearing on the development of self; the other loses itself in a great work. The theory of self-development as the great end of life, Lotze has said, is fundamentally deficient in submission and self-sacrifice; and it assuredly cannot escape a certain repulsiveness even when adopted in great earnestness by a man of such will and genius as Goethe. One may seek his moral and spiritual salvation in real selfishness. But more than this is true. If action is of central importance, the theory is wrongly based psychologically. One cannot win either the highest character or the largest happiness, with self so continually in mind. It is not even enough to take on abundance of work as moral exercise or discipline, or as a help to happiness, so long as self remains continually in mind. We need not only work, but the mood of work; not only reaction on an object, but objectivity; the work must be great enough and pressing enough for us to lose ourselves in it. The action itself reaches its perfection only so; and that means that thought and purpose and feeling, also, come to their perfection only so. Selfishness—even of the most exalted type—and introspection, in their very nature, spoil the mood of work, and make impossible the best attainment in character and the highest happiness.

One other consideration leads to the same insistence upon objectivity as an essential condition of both character and happiness. Love is both the all-inclusive virtue, and the greatest source of happiness. Neither character, then, nor happiness can be self-centered; for genuine love lives in its object, forgets itself in that, is wholly objective. Its mood, therefore, is that of the most perfect work. "By throwing their whole nature into the interests of others," Lecky justly says, "men most effectually escape the melancholy of introspection; the horizon of life is enlarged; the development of the moral and sympathetic feelings chases egotistic cares."[1]

It is true that this line of thought tends to reverse much of ordinary thought as to the predominant place of introspection and self-examination in the moral and religious life; and yet, there seems ample psychological ground for insisting that the prevailing mood must be objective. Introspection has its undoubted place, but it is a much more limited place than is ordinarily recognized.

[1] *Op. cit.*, p. 34.

Just so much introspection is valuable as may make a man sure that he is putting himself persistently in the presence of the great objective interests and personalities that make for character. When he has made himself sure upon this point, the less he thinks about himself, the better.

It needs only a word to show that this self-forgetful mood of objectivity is as valuable an element in the highest *influence*, as in character and happiness. A man counts with us, in fact, in direct proportion — other things being equal — to our confidence in his own downright conviction and disinterestedness — the degree in which he shows that he so believes in his cause or in his friend as to have quite forgotten himself in them. The attraction of such a leader is genuine and quite irresistible. He rings true and really counts. The wiliest schemes of designing men are often brought quickly to naught by the straight, sincere word or deed of a truly self-forgetful man.

Character, then, and happiness, and influence, all alike, require objectivity — self-forgetfulness — as a prime condition. And this mood, we are never to forget, is immediately connected with that persistent putting of ourselves in the presence of the great objective truths and forces and persons, for which, as we have seen, positive self-control imperatively calls. It is just here that the importance of environment in all social betterment lies. For character, and for the highest happiness as well, we *need* truths and causes and persons great enough, that in devotion to them we may lose ourselves with joy. We are thus brought to see, also, that work — the highest expressive activity — is a chief means to character and happiness and influence.

IV. WORK A CHIEF MEANS TO CHARACTER AND HAPPINESS AND INFLUENCE

If we are made for action, then we shall nowhere come to our best without work. We are made for activity, not idleness. And work, that means, not empty leisure, is chiefly to be coveted; for work is one of our greatest educators and one of our greatest joys, as the history of the race proves. Again, if even thought and feeling tend to action, and are normally complete only when the act follows, much more must this be true of the mind's active functions — volitions — and most of all of the highest volitions — moral and religious purposes. One inexorable law rules throughout: *That which is not expressed dies.* If there is, therefore, within one any desire, thought, feeling, or purpose, that he would kill, he must simply deny it all expression; it will die, — though a merely negative method here, too, may not wholly succeed. On the other hand, if there is anything he wishes to have live, he must express it. If we would have our purposes mean anything, we must put them into act. They are hardly ours at all until they are expressed. Wundt gives an interesting illustration of this law, in both its negative and positive aspects, in speaking of "the rules of good manners and of social intercourse." "Their repression of the outward signs of inconsiderate selfishness, and their constant emphasis of regard for others as the norm of social demeanor, give them a lasting control over the *inward disposition*. More urgently, because more unremittingly, than sermons on morality and disquisitions on the moral law, they exhort every one of us to leave selfishness, and respect his neighbor's rights."[1]

[1] *Op. cit.*, p. 226.

This law calls, thus, not simply for activity of some sort, but for work that shall be an expression of our best self in the full range of our being. So Höffding says: "If the action to which the purpose is directed is to be a complete expression of self, then the idea of it must be brought into inter-action with every important side of the self, that it may be made the object of a universal debate in consciousness . . . by which mere purpose becomes *resolve*."[1] Mere activity, then, is not enough. It is quite possible to overdo, for example, the emphasis on athletics and sport. They have their important and undoubted place, especially in furnishing healthful exercise and an innocent outlet for superabundant energy; but they can never take the place, even for happiness, of real work that is largely expressive of the whole self.[2] We have some need to heed a recent warning: "We live—to sum up the situation—in a generation that has gone recreation-mad. . . In all classes, high and low, veneered and unveneered, it is almost universally true that the foundations of appetite are too often laid in the struggle to 'have a good time.' The instrument of an occasional

[1] *Op. cit.*, p. 328.
[2] *Cf.* Lecky, *Op. cit.*, pp. 240 ff.

hilarity has an unfortunate tendency to develop into the minister to a quenchless thirst."[1]

It is possible to be idly busy, or at least to be busy to small purpose. The great temptation, probably, of all executives, for example, is to allow the day to be filled with many small details, and not to hold themselves to any solid large piece of work—to the work that shall call out their best and largest—to the work that is really laid upon them to do. "In the self-reverence for work, divinely commissioned, one must not hesitate to refuse 'the devastator of a day.'" Indeed, executives peculiarly need Hilty's advice: "Limit yourself to that which you really know and which has been specially committed to your care." "One must not permit himself to be overburdened with superfluous tasks."

Plainly, only through work that is some real expression of our largest self can there come to us in full measure either character or happiness or influence. Carlyle seems to have all three in mind, and the law of expression upon which they so largely depend, when he urges so impatiently: "Produce! Produce! Were it but the pitifullest. infinitesimal fraction of a product,

[1] *Atlantic Monthly*, August, 1904, p. 247.

produce it in God's name! 'Tis the utmost thou hast in thee: out with it then. Up! Up!" No mere "truth-hunting," no speculation, no high emotions, no dreams, no raptures, no thrills, no beatific vision, no transcendental revelation of the divine, no tasting God, being drunk with God, or absorption in God (as the old mystics variously put it) will avail anything, if they do not mean better character, shown in more active service. They all need active valuable expression. The biblical vision is always an appeal—"What doest thou here, Elijah?" And it calls for an answer, "Here am I; send me." There is no transfiguration scene that allows a tarrying in the mount. This holds, once again, not only for character, but, because of our very constitution, for the highest happiness and influence as well.

It is quite in harmony with the psychological emphasis we are now considering, that perhaps the most notable thing in Carl Hilty's *Happiness: Essays on the Meaning of Life*, should be a like insistence upon the need of useful work, and suggestions concerning it. "The whole nature of man," he says, "is created for activity, and Nature revenges herself bitterly on him who would rashly defy this law." "The happiest workmen are those who can absolutely lose themselves in their work." And so he urges upon young men: "Do your work from a sense of duty, or for love of what you are doing, or for love of certain definite persons; attach yourself to some great interest of human life." And he significantly adds later: "Only one must guard against making of work an idol, instead of serving God through one's work."[1]

One of the profoundest needs of our nature, thus, is work—work great enough and significant enough to call out our full powers and to absorb us. No man can afford to spare the joy of noble work, or the character and influence that are wrought out in complete self-forgetfulness in work. Surely that man will count most as a leader in a great cause, who shows that he has forgotten himself in the cause. "Get work," the great apostle of work said; "blessed is the man who has found his work, let him ask no other blessedness." "The best way to live well," Granville says, "is to work well."

In the moral development of the race, it should be noticed, the conception of work has greatly changed, until, as Wundt says,

[1] Hilty, *Happiness*. Translated by Francis G. Peabody, pp. 6, 9, 13, 92.

"the highest form of human activity is now not simply an agreeable exercise of the bodily and mental powers, but — like the humblest work that ministers to the necessities of life — conscientious fulfilment of duty. But it has not, therefore, lost the pleasurable effect that constituted its old-world attraction. On the contrary, it has communicated something of its own attractiveness to the lower forms of labor, in direct proportion as these have grown to be free manifestations of men's powers, instead of the grudging outcome of fear and coercion."[1] "Man grows with greatness of his purposes."

The need of work in which one can forget himself, thus, does not mean a dissatisfied romantic longing for some work which we count great, but from which the Divine Providence has shut us out. "Men let slip their own birthright," another has wisely said, "while they are staring enviously at their neighbor's. By a perverse ingenuity they persist in placing their ideal outside their own possibilities." Our work, the great work for us, is exactly that task given us of God — the working out of the full possibilities of our nature and of that situation in

[1] *Op. cit.*, p. 208.

which we are placed. There can be no "blue-rose melancholy" here. To no man is given a greater work than simply to do the will of God. To take up our situation and our work as given us of God is to make both great. This is the sphere of the highest heroism. Not the size of the task, but the spirit shown in the task, is the measure of the man. Tolstoi and Stevenson and Kipling, and many another, have given us great revelations of the heroism hidden under common toil. "It was left," Wundt says, "for the present age to spread the glamour of poetry little by little over all departments of life. Modern art has found a moral and æsthetic value in every form of earnest discharge of duty, and, itself the result of a changed view of life, has thus helped on its part to extend and establish the new order."[1]

This is a natural part of the Christian possibility. Every spiritual leader must be a seer of the value of the common. We all need the lesson of Robert Herrick's novel, *The Common Lot*, as he voices it in Helen's words to her husband, who had been intoxicated with the ambition for a false suc-

[1] *Op. cit.*, p. 213.

cess: "We are all trying to get out of the ranks, to leave the common work to be done by others, to be leaders. We think it a disgrace to stay in the ranks, to work for the work's sake, to bear the common lot, which is to live humbly and labor! Don't let us struggle that way any longer, dear. It is wrong — it is a curse. It will never give us happiness — never."

The common task — this is the work which we are to find great enough to lose ourselves in it, and this is our greatest educator under God. Gannett has put this so strongly in his famous sermon, "Blessed be Drudgery," that one is almost forced to quote him. "It is because we have to go, and go, morning after morning, through rain, through shine, through toothache, headache, heartache, to the appointed spot, and do the appointed work; because, and only because, we have to stick to that work through the eight or ten hours, long after rest would be so sweet; because the schoolboy's lesson must be learned at nine o'clock and learned without a slip; because the accounts on the ledger must square to a cent; because the goods must tally exactly with the invoice; because good temper must be kept with children, customers, neighbors, not seven, but seventy times seven times; because the besetting sin must be watched to-day, to-morrow, and the next day; in short, without much matter what our work be, whether this or that, it is because and only because of the rut, plod, grind, humdrum in the work, that we at last get those self-foundations laid (of which I spoke)— attention, promptness, accuracy, firmness, patience, self-denial, and the rest. When I think over that list and seriously ask myself three questions, I have to answer each with No: Are there any qualities in the list which I can afford to spare, to go without, as mere show-qualities? Not one. Can I get these self-foundations laid, save by the weight, year in, year out, of the steady pressures? No; there is no other way. Is there a single one in the list which I cannot get in some degree by undergoing the steady drills and pressures? No, not one. Then, beyond all books, beyond all class-work at the school, beyond all special opportunities of what I call my 'education,' it is this drill and pressure of my daily task that is my great schoolmaster. *My daily task*, whatever it is, *that is what mainly educates me.* All other culture is mere luxury compared with what that gives. This gives the indispensables. Yet, fool that I am, this pressure of my daily task is the very thing that I so growl at as my 'Drudgery'!"

But that which "educates me" makes *me* more — able to *be* more, to *enjoy* more, to *count* more. And Gannett's words, thus, show how indispensable some useful daily task is to us all and how great is the wrong done the child who is not held daily to some useful service. This is absolutely fundamental. For the full value of work for any of us, is to be found only in activity that seems to us worth while. If we are really made for active self-expression, we can in idleness gain happiness, as little as character or influence.[1]

This division of our inquiry ought not to be brought to a conclusion, without the emphatic caution that the insistence on the imperative need of the expression of our best selves in work does not mean any belittling of the value of a wise leisure. Fruitful leisure is rather itself the result of earnest work, and in its turn may contribute greatly to the deepening and broadening of one's work. Significant work requires the thoughtful mind that sees

[1] *Cf.* King, *Personal and Ideal Elements in Education*, pp. 119 ff.

things in their true proportions, and this demands the hours of quiet detachment from incessant activity. I should be quite unwilling to have anything that I have written regarded as an exhortation to the common nervous over-activity of Americans; for I am rather of the opinion of one of our foreign critics that "America's greatest need is repose, time to stop and take breath."

THE CONCRETENESS OF THE REAL— THE INTER-RELATEDNESS OF ALL

CHAPTER XI

THE CONCRETENESS OF THE REAL—THE PSYCHOLOGICAL EVIDENCE, CONFIRMED BY THE HISTORY OF THOUGHT

The last of the four great inferences from modern psychology is but the outcome of the three preceding. The complexity of life, the unity of man, and the importance of action alike emphasize the concrete fullness of reality. They deny that hard and fast lines can be drawn anywhere in reality, that the real can exist or be either fully conceived or stated in the abstract.

I. THE GENERAL TREND IN PSYCHOLOGY TOWARD RECOGNITION OF THIS CONCRETENESS

Not all psychologists are agreed in the individual applications of this principle, but all recognize it at many points, and the trend, I judge, is toward its universal recognition. By this it is not meant that the business of a strict scientific psychology is to interpret ideally the whole life; but that the modern psychologist, even of the atomistic school, has a wholesome and growing sense that his scientific statements of the mental process fall far short of their entire meaning. The general insistence by psychologists on the unity of the mind, and the unity of man, mind and body, already considered, is but an illustration of this growing recognition of the concreteness of reality—of relatedness everywhere. What Professor James calls the "reinstatement of the vague and inarticulate to its proper place in our mental life" means just this insistence on the relatedness of all consciousness. In our scientific work and thinking we must make use, no doubt, of many abstractions, but we must recognize at the same time, in Münsterberg's language, that they do "not reach the reality of the untransformed life."[1] The reality is always concrete. We can analyze a motion, for example, and separate from it in thought its direction and rate of speed. But there never was a real motion without a certain definite direction and rate of speed. It is interesting to notice that the *Encyclopedia Britannica* de-

[1] *Op. cit.*, p. 19.

fines a mathematical conception (which, it says, "is from its very nature abstract") as "any conception which is definitely and completely determined by means of a finite number of specifications, say by assigning a finite number of elements." This implies that the real, the concrete, cannot be so defined, can never be fully formulated. In Wundt's words: "Reality is always fuller and richer than theory."

There is within us, indeed, a constant war between the abstract and the concrete. Or, as James has suggestively put it: "Life is one long struggle between conclusions based on abstract ways of conceiving cases, and opposite conclusions prompted by our instinctive perception of them as individual facts."[1] Abstract classification is often most convenient and even necessary. And yet, so-called abstract justice—a perpetual appeal to precedent—may often be the rankest injustice; for it is likely to be mere arbitrary classing, with no recognition of individual differences, and doing away with all distinctions. Its mood, as Professor James reminds us, is essentially that of the Shah of Persia, who declined, when in England, to take any

[1] *Psychology*, Vol. II, pp. 674–675.

interest in the Derby; for he said it was already known to him that one horse could run faster than another. *Which* horse was the faster was no matter. And yet it is the individual who is the reality, and not the class. If there is any fast trotting, it is not done by the genus horse, but by some particular horse. One must therefore freely grant Professor James' contention that "the obstinate insisting that tweedledum is *not* tweedledee is the bone and marrow of life." "Life precedes, the notion follows," says Dilthey. And the notion is always less than the full life.

II. THE MIND MADE FOR RELATIONS

Enough has surely been said before, to show, also, that, just as the mind is made for action, so, too, it is made for relations. Its fundamental intellectual functions — discrimination, assimilation, and synthesis — are all relating functions, incessantly at work. And the completest intellectual counsel which can be given a man, we have seen, is: Concentrate attention upon relations. We are made for a concrete world of never-ending relations — a world in which all things are knit up indissolubly together.

III. ONE REASON FOR THE PLACE AND POWER OF ART AND LITERATURE

Here lies one of the great reasons for the place and power of art. It has an ideal, but it always presents this ideal concretely. It is no abstraction. It is so far, therefore, akin to life itself, for the very problem of life is the embodying of ideals. Art and literature, therefore, make an appeal that no abstract principle or ideal can make. We can never speak in general. We can never act in general. We can never be good in general. It is all in particulars. We have no way of expressing a general principle, but by putting it into some definite concrete individual action. Now, art and literature give us always such a concrete embodiment of an ideal, and so approach the strongest of all influences—the influence of a person.

In still another way art and literature show the power of the concrete and the individual. In his lectures on Greek sculpture, Kekule called attention to the fact that the greatest works were made for some definite purpose for a particular generation, not at all with the idea of appealing to mankind in general in all ages. But the very concreteness and definiteness of their aim—their precise adaptation to their own generation—made them all the more certain in their appeal to all men. An even more remarkable illustration is found in the Bible. Here is a book that we conceive as meant to be the spiritual guide of all men in all ages. And yet every single book in it was written with a very definite purpose to meet the exact spiritual needs of a single generation. It is this very fact that gives it its wonderful suggestion for the spiritual life.

Abstract ideals must have concrete embodiment, and that embodiment will always involve much that we would have otherwise. He who insists on confining his enthusiasm and support to the Good-in-itself and the Beautiful-in-itself—to ideal embodiments of ideals—will have no opportunities for either action or enthusiasm in this life.

IV. THE INFLUENCE OF THE IDEA OF THE ORGANISM IN THE HISTORY OF THOUGHT

The recognition of the concrete, of relatedness everywhere, has expressed itself most definitely in the history of thought, in the idea of the organism, and the attempt has been made to apply this conception not only to the individual man, but to man's relation to the world, to other men, and to God.

The Idea of the Organism before Hegel.— The classical expression of the thought as applied to society is contained in Paul's comparison of the Church to a body, in the twelfth chapter of First Corinthians. Shaftesbury is the first philosophical writer strongly to grasp the conception, and he applies it tellingly in ethics, in his *Characteristics;* and he is superficially echoed by Pope. The conception emerges anew in Kant's *Critique of Judgment*, where it is applied especially in the sphere of the beautiful. Of Kant's successors, it was emphasized particularly by Schelling, in his conception of Art and Nature, and by Schleiermacher in his æsthetic conception of religion, in his strong sense of "moral communities," as well as in his perpetual protest against all one-sidedness.

The Idea of the Organism in Hegel.— But the use of this analogy of the organism came to its climax in Hegel, whose whole philosophy it permeates. The system itself aims to be an organism, and claims as its chief justification that it is completely organic; and it strives to conceive everything organically.

Its fundamental thesis — thought and being are identical — is an assertion of so close a relation between thought and being that thought may be said to be the essence of being. His dialectical method is an attempt to formulate the process of growth of an organism, so that thinking itself, as Professor Royce has pointed out, is conceived as "a kind of living," and therefore not merely abstract. His thought that each man must repeat in his thinking the course of thought of the race, as the embryological series repeats the zoölogical, was only another application of the analogy of the organism; and he applied the conception again with special force in ethics. Even his idea of God is built upon the same analogy.

It was no accident that this philosophy gave such a spur to historical study, not indeed as a mere collecting of facts, but as a rational interpretation of events in their necessary development. Hegel's system is the best illustration of the mediating character of the philosophy of our age. It has inherited the problems of the past, and seeks to mediate between the opposing solutions — to show that the faulty solutions have all arisen from conceiving the problem too one-sidedly. That is, the Hegelian philosophy, abstract and formulizing as it is, was *intended* to be preëminently a recognition of the whole concrete reality. It aims to do justice to all, to both the real and the ideal, the individual and the whole, the sacred and the secular.

The Idea of the Organism since Hegel.—This growing recognition of the concrete is seen in the reaction from Hegel, in the interests of full reality—as against abstract *a priori* speculation—with the immensely increased attention to natural science, and, in philosophical lines, to the history of philosophy, psychology, ethics, and sociology. The Hegelians themselves show this reaction in their universal refusal to make any strict use of Hegel's formal dialectic. This tendency, in itself inevitable, has, no doubt, been confirmed and greatly strengthened by the definite setting forth of a scientific *evolution* theory, with its attempt, in the thought of an organic growth, to draw everything within its sphere. Precisely similar phenomena are the application to well nigh every subject of study of the biological or historical or "genetic," or "functional" method, as well as the present emphasis on sociology, with its assertion of the organic nature of society.

Professor Dewey's statement of a truly genetic method of treatment, perhaps, carries the idea of the organic as far as it is possible to carry it, and is itself, in his notable use of it, a striking example of the relatedness and concreteness of all reality. "The method," he says, "as well as the material, is genetic when the effort is made to see just *why and how* the fact shows itself, what is the state out of which it naturally proceeds, what the *conditions* of its manifestation, how it came to be there anyway, and what other changes it arouses or checks after it comes to be there." "For in a truly genetic method, the idea of genesis looks both ways; this fact is itself generated out of certain conditions, and in turn tends to generate something else."[1]

The whole recent "pragmatic" movement, indeed, with which both Professor Dewey and Professor James have been so closely connected, may be regarded as a kind of final stage in this development of the idea of the organic, and, at the same time, as strongly asserting both of our last two great inferences from modern psychology; as may be seen, perhaps, from Professor Bawden's

[1] In Introduction to Irving King's *The Psychology of Child Development*, pp. xiii, xv.

rather technical summary of the main positions of the movement. "The general movement," he says, "which rightly or wrongly is coming to be designated as pragmatism is away from an intellectualistic and transcendental, toward a voluntaristic and empirical metaphysics. It is thoroughly evolutionistic in its general presuppositions, though critical in its exposition of details of this doctrine. And, finally, it seeks to interpret in dynamic and functional terms the valuable results of the analysis of consciousness which the structural psychology has given us, and turns, for its basic principles of interpretation, to psychogenetic science."[1]

V. A NEW PROTEST CONSTANTLY NEEDED IN THE INTEREST OF THE WHOLE MAN

All these tendencies in the general history of thought, thus briefly passed in review, are in harmony with the psychological trend, and are so many assertions that all reality must be conceived as concretely as possible. But not only philosophy, but all our thinking —for the very reason that it is finite and

[1] *The Journal of Philosophy, Psychology, and Scientific Methods*, August 4, 1904, p. 427.

seeks to formulate the universe in intellectual terms—is likely to be too abstract—too one-sided—to be unjust to feeling, to will, and to the æsthetic, the ethical, and the religious ideals. That is, it is most likely to minimize, if not to ignore, those portions of life that refuse to be adequately formulated in intellectual terms. Even here one need not arbitrarily limit thought, but may cherish earnestly Hegel's ideal, that thinking itself is to be a kind of living, and so hope that, in the long reflection of the philosopher and in the insights of the artist and poet, thought may more and more nearly approach an adequate expression of reality; but the danger of one-sidedness and of mere intellectualism is a real one, and a new protest is therefore constantly needed in the interests of the whole concrete reality, and particularly of the whole man.

It is such a protest that is refreshingly made by Münsterberg in his *Psychology and Life*, which is not less refreshing that I do not believe it is possible in one's ultimate philosophy to keep as absolutely distinct, as he tries to do, mechanical explanation and ideal interpretation. "We are not merely passive subjects with a world of conscious objects," he says; "we are willing subjects, whose acts of will have not less reality in spite of the fact that they are no objects at all." "The reality of the will and feeling and judgment does not belong to the describable world, but to a world which has to be appreciated; it has to be linked, therefore, not by the categories of cause and effect, but by those of meaning and value."

The Protest in the History of Literature.—It is the repetition of the same protest for the whole reality that has constituted the periods of literature, as Howells has pointed out. Romanticism was a protest against the barren formalism of a decadent classicism—a demand that literature must return to the fullness and richness of life. When Romanticism came only to dream dreams and to build castles in the air, and so got away from the realities of life, Realism came in as another protest for the whole real life. The new Symbolism seems to be a kind of new protest against a barren recital of facts, while ignoring their meaning for life. Every reformation in literature, thus, as in Philosophy, is a protestantism —a protest against a one-sided viewing of life—a realism. Leslie Stephen's theory of literary development involves much the same emphasis, for it insists that the vital literature of any period must be a genuine expression of the profoundest life of that period. "The watchword of every literary school," he says, "may be brought under the formula, 'Return to Nature'; though Nature receives different interpretations." Literature must express "the really vital and powerful currents of thought which are molding society. The great author must have a people behind him; utter both what he really thinks and feels and what is thought and felt most profoundly by his contemporaries."

The Protest in Philosophy.—The severest critics of Hegel have really criticized him in that he did not carry out his own demand. He draws a sharp and unwarranted line, for example, between the analytical understanding and the unity-seeking reason. That the analogy of the organism so fully satisfies him, and is so constantly returned to, even where it has been declared insufficient, is itself a failure to follow his own principle; for the organism (though doubtless our best material symbol) can never fully express the significance of personal relations; he consequently underestimates the personal, gives no sufficient place to feeling and will, and therefore belittles the ethical, and for both reasons fails to understand the real and permanent significance of the historical. No principle less broad than that of the whole spirit can be made to interpret spirit.

The Protest in History.—But does not the immense influence of the evolution theory in all subjects of inquiry, and the well-nigh universal use of the biological or historical method show that the analogy of the organism *is* sufficient for the spiritual as well as for the natural sciences? Do not both classes of sciences use the same method? In a broad sense, no doubt, both these implied statements are true. The methods of natural science and of history never so nearly approached each other as today, and both do aim to trace a growth. But it is still true that personal relations cannot be adequately expressed by the organic, and that the *aims* and *interests* of the methods of the natural sciences and of history are different.

Windelband seems to me to state the contrast not too strongly, in his Rector's address before the University of Strassburg, when he says: "The empirical sciences (including natural science and history) seek in the knowledge of the actual (1) either the universal in the form of law, or (2) the individual in its historically determined shape; they look, on the one hand, to the ever identical form, and, on the other, to the unique self-determined content of the actual occurrence. The former are sciences of law, the latter sciences of events; the one teach what always is; the other what once was." If this distinction is a true one, the aim and interest of the two classes of science are quite different. The scientist is interested in a particular phenomenon only as an illustration of the universal—of law; the historian is interested in his individual phenomenon, as individual, for what it is in itself.

It is in exactly this sense, I suppose, that Münsterberg says: "The appreciation of a physical object as a whole is never natural science, and the interpretation and suggestion of a mental state as a whole is never psychology" (in the strictest scientific sense).[1] Now, the universal — the law — is of great value for human knowledge, but only as it helps us,— to quote another—"by reasoning, to know new truths about individual things." In itself it is no reality; "the things of worth are all concretes and singulars."[2] "In the unique-

---
[1] *Op. cit.*, p. 149.
[2] James, *Psychology* Vol. I, p. 479.

ness, the incomparability of the object," says Windelband, "root all our feelings of worth."

It is only the natural-scientific point of view, therefore, that sees in the individual members of the development series but transient stages—steps in the process; the true historical point of view abides by the concrete individual, and holds that the historical is itself of essential significance. It was in this sense, I suppose, that Harnack said, that although biography was the least scientific, it was at the same time the most valuable history. In the study of the single life, that is, it was least possible to trace exact causal connections; but in so far as the meaning and spirit of this individual life were reached, the study yielded the greatest value. So Höffding says: "Each individual trait, each individual property, might perhaps be explained by the power of heredity and the influence of experience; but the inner unity, to which all elements refer, and by virtue of which the individuality is a *psychical* individuality, remains for us an eternal riddle." "Psychical individuality is one of the practical limits of science."[1]

The tendency to recognize the whole con-

[1] *Op. cit.*, pp. 353, 354.

crete reality, therefore, leads of itself to an emphasis on the historical as such, and not merely as illustrating general principles. This is the point of Lotze's emphatic protest: "And therefore will we always combat these conceptions which acknowledge only one-half, and that the poorer half, of the world; only the unfolding of facts to new facts, of forms to new forms, and not the continual mental elaboration of all these outward events into that which alone in the universe has worth and truth—into the bliss and despair, the admiration and loathing, the love and the hate, the joyous certainty and the despairing longing, and all the nameless fear and favor in which that life passes which alone is worthy to be called life."[1]

The Protest in Education.—The protest in education in the interest of the whole man cannot be less earnest than the protest in literature or philosophy or history. All that psychology has to say as to the unity of man shows the absurdity of exclusive tendencies in any education that really looks to life. The protest is needed, and in part at least made, all along the line; but nowhere is it needed more than in public school and

[1] *Microcosmus*, Vol. II, p. 167.

in college education. Whatever is true as to other parts of our educational system, here surely, the interests of the whole man demand attention, and in definite, concrete ways.[1] And much of the most sound and wholesome educational counsel of our time connects itself directly with this emphasis of modern psychology upon the concreteness of reality and so upon the whole man.

VI. THE EMPHASIS ON PERSONS AND PERSONAL RELATIONS — THE SOCIAL SELF

It is evident that the justification of the historical, of which we have spoken, rests on a belief in the absolute worth of the person. The emphasis on the historical, therefore, becomes an emphasis on the person and personal relations, on the social self — on the entire experience of the entire soul in its relations to others. The fundamental convictions of the social consciousness must be, thus, ultimately involved in the emphasis upon the concrete. The historical point of view agrees with the natural-scientific — in its assertion of relatedness everywhere (and its consequent use of the

[1] *Cf.* King, *Personal and Ideal Elements in Education*, pp. 13 ff.

idea of evolution), but adds an equally emphatic insistence on the concrete individual. At first sight this seems like denying all divisions, on the one hand, and asserting them on the other. Yet relatedness and personality are not opposed. "To be," Lotze says, "is to be in relations." But he makes it the fundamental proposition of his spiritualism that only spirits are capable of entering into relations. Certainly, the emphasis on the concreteness of all reality must be an emphasis not only upon the permanent significance of the historical as such, but also upon the surpassing significance of persons and personal relations. As Brierley says of literature, "The personal is the one thing that interests. Doctrine and dogma, whether theologic, social, or economic, left to its naked self, will moulder on the back shelves of libraries. To be powerful, it must be incarnated."[1]

Even more than that we are made for action, is it true, that we are persons and are made for personal relations; and these personal relations are a part of our very being.

The Human Body Looks to Personal Association. — Even our bodies show that we are

[1] *Studies of the Soul*, p. 25.

made for personal association. No animal body approaches man's in the free use of the arms as instruments of work, or, especially because of the uncovered skin of man, in the speaking power of his countenance. And in just the degree in which our bodies are made for work which reveals ourselves, and in just the degree in which our bodies are capable of expressing our inner life and each feature of it with fine adaptation, in just that degree are we fitted even as to body in superior measure for personal association. The long and helpless infancy of the human being, moreover, compels the development of love and care, if the race is to continue at all. Here, too, the very bodily organization of man shuts him up to personal association.

The Witness of Infancy.—The earliest days of life, too, are a witness that we are made for personal relations. The child knows persons before he knows things, Dilthey believes; and this is most significant. "The foundation for our whole social consciousness," says Royce, "seems to lie in certain instincts which characterize us as social beings, and which begin to assume considerable prominence toward the end of the first year of an infant's life." "Our social environment," he adds, "is a constant source of numerous sensory pleasures, and by association becomes interesting to us accordingly. But in addition to the pleasures of sense which are due to our human companions, there are, no doubt, from the first, deep instinctive and hereditary sources of interest in the activities of human beings."[1] As to later childhood, Dawson says, as the outcome of an extended investigation: "At all ages children feel more interested in *persons* than in any other elements of the Bible."[2]

The Witness of the Moral History of the Race.—The history of the moral development of the race compels us to lay the same emphasis upon personal association. The general humanistic spirit has only through it come into being. As Wundt says, "there were two principal causes that led up to it, *friendship* and *hospitality*—forms of personal relation through which the more general humanistic idea gradually attained to maturity." And Wundt finds, moreover, in the moral development of the race, "two fundamental *psychological motives*, whose universal validity de-

[1] *Outlines of Psychology*, p. 275.
[2] Quoted by Du Bois, *The Natural Way*, p. 249.

pends upon the constancy with which they produce their effect in human consciousness: the feelings of *reverence* and of *affection*." "The whole development of morality," he says, "rests on the expression of these two fundamental impulses of human nature."[1] It would be difficult to state more strongly the fundamental character of personal association for the life of men.

The Witness of Philosophy.—It is a remarkable thing, too, that, though a denial of the external world is common enough among philosophers, no philosopher has ever denied the existence of other persons. The philosopher seems, rather, compelled to accept persons as indubitable facts. Persons are for us, in truth, the most real of realities—the most certain and the most important facts. No factors in our environment are so mighty as the personal factors; no relations so decisive. And personal relations are really more clear to our understanding, even, than any of the analogies from things by which we strive to illustrate them. We know them better. Here has lain the folly of religious thinking (repeated over and over)—in trying to express the profoundest personal relations

[1] *Op. cit.*, pp. 283, 328.

within the terms of impersonal analogies. The history of theology is full of such futile attempts.

The Whole Man Revealed Only in Personal Relations.— Moreover, the real man — the entire man — is revealed only in personal relations. All that he is comes out only here — not in what he says, not even in what he does. It is in the relation of man to man that he stands fully revealed. The great desideratum, therefore, is not complete knowledge about a man, but acquaintance with him, in which there comes to us more of impression, of feeling, of impulse, of inspiration, of contagion of character, than any formula we make can express. We are continually made conscious of the fact that we cannot *tell* another all our friend means; the other must find him out only in a personal association of his own.

So Birrell finds Charles Lamb revealed in his personal relation to his father: "In early manhood," he says, "Coleridge planned a Pantisocracy where all the virtues were to thrive. Lamb did something far more difficult: he played cribbage every night with his imbecile father, whose constant stream of querulous talk and fault-finding might well have goaded a far stronger man into practising and justifying neglect." And Birrell quotes from a significant letter of Lamb's to Coleridge: "O my friend, cultivate the filial feelings; and let no man think himself released from the kind charities of relationship: these shall give him peace at last; these are the best foundation for every species of benevolence. I rejoice to hear that you are reconciled with all your relations." It is the great theme of Maurice's *Social Morality*, that the common personal relations of life are precisely the great means of the divine training. Only in personal relations is the whole being brought out.

This is the real and eternal truth in mysticism which makes it recur after every period of rationalism. It is not necessarily mistiness nor an avoidance of clear thinking, but it is a deep conviction that things are more than we can tell; that only an abstract conception can be fully formulated, the concrete individual, never. Life is always more than thought; the concrete, than the abstract. The whole man is more than any possible intellectual formula for him. We can experience and feel and do and live more than we can tell. The entire man is the reality, the intellect alone is the abstraction. The truest realism, therefore, is emphasis on the whole personal life, and so final mysticism; and mysticism that really understands itself must be realism.[1] To similar import, Professor Coe says of the modern conception of the religious life: "We have not to ask men to take into themselves something foreign to their nature. Our invitation is rather this: 'Be your whole self! Be completely in earnest with your intellectual sincerity, with your conscientiousness, with your love of fellow-men, with your aspiration for all that is true and beautiful and good, and you will find that a sense of God is the moving spring of the whole.' "[2]

[1] *Cf.* King, *Theology and the Social Consciousness*, Chapters V–VI.
[2] *The Religion of a Mature Mind*, pp. 248–249.

CHAPTER XII

THE CONCRETENESS OF THE REAL—SUGGESTIONS FOR LIVING

I. RESPECT FOR THE LIBERTY AND THE PERSONALITY OF OTHERS

THIS emphasis on the concrete and personal suggests at once a third great condition for character and happiness and influence, besides self-control and objectivity—sacred respect for the liberty and the personality of others.[1]

Recognition of the Moral Freedom of Others.—For, in the first place, all that is best in us can only *become;* it must be from within; as Miss Brackett says of rest—it cannot be pasted on to one. The springs and the essential conditions of character and happiness and influence are inner; and there must be left, therefore, to every person a very genuine and inviolable sphere of freedom. Even in the case of a child, it is recognized that this

[1] *Cf.* Patterson Du Bois, *The Natural Way*, Chapter III; King, *The Appeal of the Child*, pp. 24 ff.

sphere of freedom should enlarge as the child grows. Sully rightly warns: "Nothing is more fatal to will-growth than an excess of discipline permeating the whole of a child's surroundings." "Play," he says, "owes no little of its moral value to the fact that it provides this area of unrestricted activity." It isn't best that all play should be under even kindergarten instruction; though Froebel meant exactly to guard against this overriding of the child, in seeking always "a development from within, never a prescription from without."

Increasingly, counsel, friendly suggestion, or unspoken influence must replace command. There can be no character otherwise; for character must be one's own creation. The wise teacher or parent aims to produce not a mere going through the motions of right conduct, not certain objective results, certain outward performances, but an inner life, that can be a genuine source of character and happiness and influence, that shall be *in* the child a spring of water, bubbling up into life. No one is established in real character—and so in happiness and influence—in whom there is not the inner desire and purpose of righteous living, as well as the corresponding forms of conduct. The conduct must be our own, chosen with living volition, if it is to mean character. And if work is to give us joy, it must not be merely compelled, but taken on as possibility of genuine attainment and conquest. Patterson Du Bois has so perfectly expressed the true attitude here, in his contrast between the old and the new conceptions of fatherhood, that I can do no better than to quote him. The true father, he maintains, says not, "I will conquer that child whatever it costs *him*," but, "I will help that child to conquer himself, whatever it costs *me*." And that attitude will require, throughout, a sacred respect for the child's own liberty. It *is* quite possible, in this sense, to tie a boy disastrously to his mother's apron-strings. It is imperative that the boy should be brought to decisions of his own —not merely going through the motions of his mother's decisions. This is the secret of the fatal weakness of character often shown by over-trained children. On the other hand, the true conception is indicated by Dr. Matheson: "The dearest moment to the heart of a parent is the moment of a child's spontaneity—the day when it anticipates the ordinary command and does the deed of its own accord."[1] For this means moral insight and choice on the child's own part.

Recognition of the Sacredness of the Person.—But there must be more than a merely formal perception that the other man is a free being. There must be a real recognition of the sacredness of the person, of the inviolable right to his own individuality. "For there is a modesty of the soul as well as of the body," and an individuality that ought to be respected both by others and by the individual himself. In Brierley's words, "each soul God creates has its own flavor, and we want to taste that flavor. When the young worker has learned precisely what he is as distinguished from others, and gives us that in whatever limited quantity, or sphere of operation, he becomes valuable."[2]

The very possibility of character involves that in a very real sense *every person is*—what Kant called him—*an end in himself*. He does not exist simply for another—this would make him a thing; and it is the essence of slavery, it has been often said, to treat a person as a thing. The one absolutely damning and deadly thing in all personal relations

[1] Quoted by Du Bois, *Op. cit.*, p. 294.
[2] *Studies of the Soul*, p. 127.

is the spirit of contempt. No relation can be what it ought to be where this spirit is present. The employer must respect his workmen; the mistress her maid; the speaker his audience; the teacher his pupils; the parent his child. And this means that one must seek to be continually at his own best, and must persistently aim to get at the other's best. Any other attitude simply cultivates distrust by others and distrust of others that sap both happiness and influence.

In every child lie the possibilities of character and happiness and influence. His destiny is his own; his choices his own. Beyond a certain pretty definite limit no man can go; but far short of that lies a limit beyond which no man — not even the parent — has a right to go. One of my friends has never been able to forget the sense of personal outrage she felt as a little child, when her mother, without her consent, took the key and went through a little doll's chest of drawers that had been given her as her own. There was nothing she cared specially to hide from her mother, but she felt that her mother had unwarrantably invaded her privacies; that her consent should have been at least asked. And I suspect the child was right. Conspicuously "capable" and strong-willed mothers are particularly likely to err here — they know so well exactly what it is best that every member of their households should wear and say and do. They are benevolent tyrants. Now, one of the inalienable rights of every living being is the right to make at least some blunders of his own. And it is better that the daughter should not always dress most becomingly than that she should never have opportunity to make decisions of her own; the decisions, indeed, must often be laid upon her, even against her desire.

And this counsel has its application in all personal relations. The strong-willed need here to be constantly on their guard. Some natures seem essentially tyrannical everywhere, even in their closest friendships. They may be very devoted, but they have no respect for the liberty or individuality of others; and they have forgotten Miss Yonge's penetrating remark: "It is a great thing to sacrifice; but it is a greater, to consent not to sacrifice in one's own way." These omniscient friends, who know so much better than one does himself what is good for him, and who insist upon his enjoying himself in the ways they have prescribed, it must be confessed, are something of a trial. The "exploiter of souls," as Mrs. Deland deftly names this type, though often possessed of some lovely traits, is truly not *altogether* lovely.

Masterful races are likewise tempted, in dealing with other peoples, to overlook the peculiar individual contributions and enjoyments and points of view of those peoples, and to insist on making them happy and prosperous in the fashion of the conquerors. Star differs from star in glory; and "the white man's burden" may be undertaken in quite too conceited and contemptuous a spirit. That "certain blindness in human nature," of which Professor James speaks so effectively, shuts us out inevitably from the best relations to others.[1] One may not interfere to the extent of his power in either the character or the happiness of another, however close to one the other may be. Here lies, too, the fundamental psychological error of all communistic schemes.

It is worth noticing that Paul's single counsel, as I have elsewhere pointed out,[2] concerning the training of children, subtly

---
[1] *Talks on Psychology, and Life's Ideals*, pp. 229 ff.
[2] *The Appeal of the Child*, pp. 24 ff.

grows out of this very principle, "Fathers, provoke not your children to wrath." Don't trespass on the child's personality. Respect the person.

We cannot make people enlightened, or good, or happy, by compulsion (though this does not mean that we are not to do all we can to make their environment wholesome and uplifting). So Erdmann says, with true insight, of the enlightened despotism of Frederick the Great, whose principle was that "the unenlightened must be compelled to be rational and happy": "He came to know with sorrow that those who had shaken off their prejudices at his command remained in bondage *to him*. The forty-six years of their greatest king furnished perhaps the main reason why the Prussian people were for so many years destitute of enthusiasm, and therefore of capacity, for self-government."[1] One must sacredly respect the personality of another. One must believe in other men — genuinely respect them — if he is to influence them in a finally high and wholesome way. The cynic cuts himself off, from the beginning, from the best and largest influence upon others. This

[1] *History of Philosophy*, Vol. II, p. 304.

deep and true estimate of others, moreover, is the only road to a genuine, not a false, humility.

Many a Friendship Is Hurt by This Lack of Respect.—The delicate bloom of the grape will not bear much handling. There are limitations to all intimacies; let us not forget it. I am not to presume in my friendships; I am not to pry; I am not to scold; I am not to take away the possibility of decision or choice, even with a child. My child will best learn respect for personality from my treatment of him. I am not to insist on the explanation by my friend of every mood. Every soul must in much be alone and ought to be. One only degrades his friendships when he measures them by the number of liberties he takes, the number of privacies he rides over roughshod. In all friendship, one is to ask, not demand; the door must be opened from within, it must not be forced from without. The secrets of friendship (like those of the Lord) are always with those who fear. Those reverent of personality shall alone see either God or the best in man. A high-minded man can reveal himself only to the reverent. So Granger says: "The spirit does not entrust its deeper inspirations unless to those who can guard them."[1] Our feeling in this respect is not likely to be too delicate. Like the Christ in Revelation, we are to stand at the door of the heart only to knock. We may well cultivate the reverence which Goethe makes the essence of religion —reverence for that which is above us, for that which is beside us, for that which is beneath us. After all, the only really sacred thing is a person, and the sacredness of all places and things is borrowed from persons. The teaching of Christ has as a foundation-stone such a reverence for personality—reverence for man as man because each is a child of God.

Moreover, the truest development in civilization is to be seen only in this deepening sense of the sacredness of the person. There is *no higher test of the civilization* of any community or nation. A nation's treatment, thus, of its women and children and dependents, is the surest measure of its real progress. Every step in the moral progress of the race has been a step into a growing reverence for personality. And the depth of this respect is thus a delicate measure of one's own attainment. Reverence for another, therefore, is

[1] *The Soul of the Christian*, p. 75.

essential to us, as well as to the other. "He who considers himself the Lord of others," said Fichte, "is himself a slave." The contemptuous spirit is the working of death in us. What one reckons the value of his own self to be, what his own claim on life is—this is necessarily his standard for the respect due to others. Reverence for personality is thus a kind of guide for love itself. The meaning of the Golden Rule to any man depends on how much the self means to him. The most searching questions a man can put to himself, therefore, are just these: How deep and sacred a thing to me is a person? How significant is friendship?

II. THE POWER OF PERSONAL ASSOCIATION

This emphasis on the concrete and the personal also suggests a second great means to happiness, to character, and to influence—personal association.

Influence of Imitation.—The enormous influence of imitation, in the development of the individual, upon which, as we have seen, both Baldwin and Royce lay such emphasis, points at once to the primary importance of personal association. And it holds for the entire range of human activities, even the purely intellectual. Thus Sully points out, for example: "A child will profit more by daily companionship with an acute observer, be he teacher or playfellow, than by all systematic attempts to train the senses."[1] "The deepest spring of action in us is the sight of action in another," James says. "The spectacle of effort is what awakens and sustains our own effort." One of the most valuable and promising recent gains in the educational life of the country is the tendency to make much more of the distinctly social possibilities of our public schools. We can spare nowhere the power of personal association.

One Must Be Won to Character.—Again, just because character is what it is, and must have liberty as a condition, its great *means*, for ourselves and others, cannot be force, precept, or command, but the winning to a free choice—to an inner response. One must be attracted toward it. For it can come only of our own will. And attraction is precisely what occurs in personal association. Similarly, since happiness cannot be commanded, but comes only on conditions which are inner even more than outer, these conditions are

[1] *Op. cit.*, p. 214.

likely to be preëminently personal. And of influence, it is manifestly true that its very possibility depends upon the fact that we are members one of another; and one's influence, therefore, will count in direct proportion as the laws of personal association are carefully observed.

We Are Made for Personal Relations.—But it is chiefly just because we are personal and made for personal relations that we may be sure that the chief means to character and happiness and influence is personal association. Character is caught, not taught, and happiness and influence have their highest source in friendship. This emphasis upon the fact that character comes rather by contagion than by teaching, is, of course, not intended to deny the moral value of insight, for this is involved in the very unity of the mind, already dwelt upon.[1] But, as Du Bois says, here "our need is less a matter of direct teaching and preaching than of atmospheric influence—example, suggestion, pure speech, gentle manner, sweet temper, strong handling, firm stepping in virtue."[2] Indeed, the child rather resents direct moralizing; and

---
[1] *Cf.* Paulsen, *A System of Ethics*, pp. 26, 40, 58, etc.
[2] *The Natural Way*, p. 137.

the insistence on drawing the moral may even distinctly lessen the power of story or example; not chiefly, I think, because moralizing is abstract, but because it seems to press in too closely and unwarrantably on the child's inner personality.[1]

One Cannot Learn to Love Alone.—Moreover, if love is the all-inclusive virtue, the highest happiness, and the highest sphere of influence, then character and happiness and influence, alike, must come chiefly in *association*. One cannot learn to love alone. We need, for our very life, much common democratic association with men. It is the business of life to learn to fulfil wisely and faithfully the common personal relations of life, and we shall not learn this in a vacuum.[2] This, some one has nobly said, "is the highest and richest education of a human nature — not an instruction, not a commandment, but a friend."

Personal Association the Greatest Means.— Leaving to one side, now, the special consideration of happiness and influence— though inferences as to both will be continually implied—let us note that, besides work, and more than work, *personal associa-*

[1] *Cf.* King, *Personal and Ideal Elements in Education*, pp. 191 ff.
[2] *Cf.* King, *Op. cit.*, pp. 112 ff.

tion is the one great hopeful means to character; and in the long run this conviction must affect profoundly all our religious conceptions.[1]

Whence come our greatest convictions, our deepest faiths? From personal associations. Personal contact and impression of character count more here than all argument. You find yourself responding like a vibrating chord to the note of your friend. His faith and life become the firmest ground for yours. You catch his conviction, his spirit. It may well be a relief to a conscientious but growing teacher, that it is not a man's individual propositions, so much as the general trend of his thinking, his spirit, his tone, his atmosphere, which remain with others. This total result now becomes in them, too, a *living germ*, going on to grow in them as in him. It is not propositions, not definitions, not demonstrations, that give inspiration, but the *touch of life*. As James says of the prophet: " Just as our courage is so often a reflex of another's courage, so our faith is apt to be, as Max Müller somewhere says, a faith in some one else's faith. We draw new life from the heroic example. The prophet has drunk

[1] *Cf.* King, *Reconstruction in Theology*, Chapters XI–XII.

more deeply than any one of the cup of bitterness, but his countenance is so unshaken and he speaks such mighty words of cheer, that his will becomes our will, and our life is kindled at his own."[1]

This is no strange thought among men who have cared for character. Even Kant, with all the rigor of his moral theory, knew that morals could be taught effectively only by example. It is quite in line with this that Professor Everett, in his *Ethics for Young People*, advises that each child should keep a book of heroes. Almost all Fichte's popular works turn upon the thought of the personal vocation of the scholar, as the great inspirer of men. Carlyle, who felt Fichte profoundly, characteristically protests against morals by argument: " Foolish word-monger and motive-grinder, that in thy logic mill hast an earthly mechanism for the Godlike itself, and would'st fain grind me out virtue from the husks of pleasure — I tell thee, Nay." "Nay," he asks, " has not, perhaps, the motive-grinder himself been in love?"

Not to mention the many names that might be added to the list, who see in per-

[1] *Psychology*, Vol. II, p. 579.

sonal association the great means to character, let me simply remind you of three characteristic and particularly notable and influential utterances of the last sixty years, published twenty years apart and yet all turning upon this single thought: Dr. Bushnell's sermon on *Unconscious Influence*, preached in 1846, that has been the inspiration of more sermons, perhaps, than any other sermon ever preached in America; Professor Seeley's *Ecce Homo*, published in 1866, with its living emphasis on Jesus' contagious "enthusiasm of humanity"; and Professor Drummond's addresses, *The Greatest Thing in the World*, and *The Changed Life*, delivered in 1889, that go deeper, perhaps, than anything else he ever wrote in the indication of the supreme method in the moral and spiritual life — changing into the image of Christ through persistent association with him. The world will not willingly let any of these die. They strike the keynote of character.

"Ideas," George Eliot says, "are often poor ghosts; our sun-filled eyes cannot discern them — they pass athwart us in their vapor, and cannot make themselves felt. But sometimes they are made flesh; they breathe upon us with warm breath, they touch us with soft responsive hands, they look at us with sad sincere eyes, and speak to us in appealing tones; they are clothed in a living human soul, with all its conflicts, its faith, and its love. Then their presence is a power, then they shake us like a passion, and we are drawn after them with gentle compulsion, as flame is drawn to flame." Münsterberg, in his *Psychology and Life*, bears the same testimony as a psychologist, in terms almost as strong. "Only a conscience which is penetrated by morality stands safe in all storms, and such a conscience is not brought out by technical prescriptions, nor by punishments and jails; no, only by the obligatory power of will upon will, by the inspiring life of subjects we acknowledge, by the example of the heroes of duty, that speaks directly from will to will, and for which we cannot substitute psychological training and police officers."[1]

> "And so the Word had breath and wrought
> With human hands the creed of creeds
> In loveliness of perfect deeds,
> More strong than all poetic thought."

Christ himself built his kingdom on twelve men, and their personal association with him.

[1] *Op. cit.*, pp. 176, 177.

Facing the whole problem of character for all his disciples in all time, he deliberately makes the one great means, personal relation to himself, not the acceptance of certain methods or principles or ideas or machinery. None of his teaching is in abstract propositions; there are no scientific definitions or demonstrations. All is immediate and vital. It is not a system, fixed and dead, but a seed of life. The most conserving and inspiring of all influences is the love of a holy person. The most effective possible way in which we can put ourselves in the presence of the great objective forces and causes and values, and be sure that our own interest and enthusiasm in them shall be keen and abiding, is through close and persistent association with those persons in whom the great values of life are already dominant. This whole psychological emphasis upon personal association, thus, drives the thoughtful man back to the supreme importance of close touch with the great persons of history and, above all, with the supreme person of history — Jesus Christ. The best can come to us only by this objective and personal method.

Upon the side of influence, of course, this

principle means that the fundamental condition must be, that we should be what we would have others become, that genuine character and conviction must be back of all expression. Ultimately, we have nothing to give to others but ourselves. There is, thus, no cheap way in which a man may count profoundly for good. He must be what he ought to be; he must aim to keep himself persistently at his best; within this limit of his persistent best he must be willing to give himself unstintedly to others, sharing, directly or indirectly, his best with them. With the young this involves patient, steady training into the loving life, putting them into some real service of others, and, so far as we can, through our honest witness and spirit, putting them in the presence of the best we ourselves have found. Even here we are not to over-moralize. Association and work are the great dependence. This is the costly way to effective living. But if the life of the loving God is also the life of supreme felicity, this costly way to influence is at the same time the royal road to happiness.

The two great psychological principles now passed in review—the central importance of action, and the emphasis on the concrete—

underlie most of the important educational counsel of our time:— (1) Express your thought or feeling, put it into act; and (2) consider the relatedness of things. Each has many applications beyond what it has been possible for me to suggest; and each should be a growing principle in every life.

The resulting suggestions for living seem to have given us the really supreme conditions and means for character, for influence, and for happiness — the supreme factors in the largest and richest life, and so of the spiritual life as well. There are many subsidiary principles. I think there are none of equal importance. The three great *conditions* are self-control, objectivity, and respect for personality; the three great *means* are the practice of self-control, work, and personal association. Of these, self-control comes back finally to the two others. When would the other conditions and means become ideal? When our work could be taken as a God-given work to which we could commit ourselves without misgiving or reserve, and in which, thus, we might lose ourselves with complete objectivity. When the personal association was with the highest—with God himself, made real and concrete to us in his character and love through the personal life of Christ, and individualized for each one in his spiritual presence in us, constant and most intimate, but unobtrusive, leaving our own liberty sacredly guarded.

Just these ideal conditions to which psychology leads us, Christ declares to be actual. His prayer for his disciples included just these two requests — for the divine association, for a God-given work: "Keep them in thy name"—in the divine association; "Sanctify them in the truth. As thou dids't send me into the world, even so send I them into the world." Set them apart even as I am set apart, unto a divinely given mission. No life can fail in character, in influence, or in happiness, for whom these two requests—with their implied self-control — are granted. To find the Great Companion, and the work he gives—this is the sum of all.

Or, to come at the matter in a slightly different way, Christ has one all-inclusive principle: life through self-sacrifice—saving the life by losing it—love. This, in his teaching, clearly means three things: habitual self-control; devotion to the work given us to do—facing exactly our situation; and giving ourselves in our personal relations to others. The corresponding moods required are: in self-control, deliberation in face of impulse; in devotion to work, objectivity; in personal association, respect for personality. Now, consecration to the will of God, as Christ conceives the matter, covers all—this supreme giving of the self including all subordinate givings. For consecration to the will of God means the willing obedience to the laws of our nature, recognized as from God—the subordination of the lower to the higher—*self-control*. It means devotion to the *work* given us to do. It means yielding to the supreme *association* with the loving God, and hence love for men. A self-sacrificing or self-giving love, thus, is for Christ the whole.

In a word, the supreme condition of love is reverence for the person, of which self-control is simply a genuine expression; and the unselfish objectivity of love is at the same time the highest mood of work. It is the faith of the Christian that, through the love of God, he is in the divine association, and set apart unto his work—sent as Christ was sent. And in this love of God for men he finds his own measure of the reverence due the person of his fellows, and so his highest motive to self-control. To him, too, it belongs to claim his part in the inheritance promised in Christ's words—"that *the love* wherewith thou lovest me may be in them"; and, in his measure, at the end to say—"Father, I have finished *the work* which thou gavest me to do." And it is impossible that one should be all he ought to be in work and association, without clear recognition of the complexity and paradoxes of life, and faithful fulfilment of the conditions involved in the unity of his nature. Our four great inferences are thus brought together into one.

INDEX

Acquaintance, a growth and active achievement, 44.

Action, and will, of central importance, 3,4; in fixing habit, 92; may not safely yield place to insights or feeling, 128; born of will, reveals man, 145; Höffding on, 145; Stanley Hall on, 145; impulse to, fundamental, 146 ff; natural terminus of every experience, 149 ff; neutral organism a machine for (James), 150; muscular system organized for, 150 ff; Professor Hall on, 150 ff; mind organized for, 153 ff; James on, 153; even necessary for thought and feeling, 154 ff; central importance of, shown in influence of practical interests, 161 ff; enormous place of, in life, 176 ff.

Activities, of mind, reciprocal, 103; Starr and Sully on harmonious development of, 103, 104; Royce on, 104 ff.

Activity, no, at its best when attention is centered on self, 192 ff; man created for, 202 ff.

Activity, intellectual, opposed functions of, 24 ff; general forms or types of, 45 ff; effect of mental, on body, 56 ff; of will on muscular, 58 ff; bodily, a contributor to spiritual and religious life, 60, 93, 100 ff; a necessity to bodily health, 65 ff; need to guard against fatigue in, 70; psychical effects of, 77 ff; imitative, in development of self-consciousness, Baldwin on, 148; need of, for inadequately trained, 151 ff; Wundt on, expressive, 157; required for growth, 158.

Adolescence. Hall on peculiar power of active instincts in, 150 ff; Lecky on, 151.

Americans, in need of warning, 76; overactivity of, 209.

Aristippus, the Cyrenaic, principle of, 182.

Aristotle, on best mental habits, 24.

Arnold, Matthew, on conduct and life, 175.

Art, has power through concrete appeal, 214.

Asceticism, ignoring of the particular, the common error of, 45; recognized bodily conditions, 47; failure of, 48; lesson of natural science concerning, 48 ff; the true place of, 93 ff; good only as means, 95; Harnack on, 97; Pfleiderer on, 98; psychological basis for, 99; Paul on the true, 99; the history of, a protest against love of ease, 101; Bishop Westcott on, 101.

Association, personal, the greatest means to happiness, character, and influence, 246 ff; greatest convictions from, 250; James on power of, 250; Bushnell, Seeley, and Drummond on, 252; George Eliot on, 252 ff; Münsterberg on, 253; Christ's example for, 253 ff; to have value, involves keeping ourselves at our best, 255.

Atlantic Monthly, referred to, 152.

Atomism, revolt against, 108.

Attention, nerve power the chief factor in, 67 ff; power of, the basis of self-control, 69, 74, 161; Mosso on, 69; opportunity for will-training in, 90; concentration of, leads to action, 153 ff; the will in, 159 ff; requires large circle of interests, 191.

Augustine, referred to, 112; quoted by Granger on definiteness in thinking, 123 ff.

Baldwin, on unity of mind and body, 63; on imitative activity, 148; law of dynamogenesis, 150; emphasis on imitation, 171; referred to, 246.

INDEX

Barnes, referred to, 162.

Barrie, quoted, 27.

Bawden, Professor, summary of "pragmatism," 219 ff.

Beard, on brain-fag, 68.

Belief, the normal state, 126.

Berkeley, referred to, 108.

Berlin, university students in, 170.

Bible, value in concreteness, 215.

Biedermann, on religion, 38.

Birrell, Augustine, on hurtful intellectual habits, 124; on Charles Lamb, 233 ff.

Bishop of Exeter, referred to, 43.

Blood, need of well-oxygenated, 64 ff; need of, for sanity, 65; Starr on, referred to, 65; Corning's experiments in circulation of, 65; Mosso's emphasis on quality of, 65; LaGrange's emphasis on, 65; fatigue, a poisoning of, 65 ff; not the chief factor in attention, 67; circulation of, looks to action, 149.

Bodily conditions, basis of true living, 48 ff; not a denial of spiritual life, 50, 53; effects of feeling on, 55; underlie character, 64, 74; in the religious life, 74 ff; a means of power, Professor Jastrow on, 78.

Bodily functions, dependent on self-control, 85.

Body, the, not evil *per se*, 94 ff; influenced by the mind, 78 ff; by joyful emotions, 135 ff; organized for action, 149 ff; looks to personal associations, 229 ff.

Bowne, referred to, 108.

Brackett, Miss, on rest, 80; on effect of painful emotion, 136; referred to, 236.

Bradley, referred to, 194.

Brain, psychical states and, 51 ff; James on, 51; effects of feeling on, 56.

Brain-fag, diminishes power of inhibition, 68; Americans peculiarly liable to, 76; prevents success, 76, 77.

Brierley, on dogma, 229; on sacredness of the person, 239.

Browning, quoted, 29, 102, 184.

Burnham, Dr. W. H., on economic brain action, 70; on effect of work on nerve-cells, 71; on the sense perceptions, 71 ff; referred to, 67.

Bushnell, referred to, 82; on unconscious influence, 252.

Butler, Bishop, referred to, 141, 154.

Cæsar, referred to, 126.

Call, Miss, referred to, 82, 83.

Carlyle, referred to, 126; Seeley on, 158; in *Sartor Resartus*, 167 ff; on work, 201 ff; on character by example, 251.

Chalmers, Dr., sermon on The Expulsive Power of a New Affection, 190.

Chamberlain, on Mosso, referred to, 67.

Character, paradox in choice of, and life-work, 31 ff; James on, 32; requires both self-assertion and self-surrender, Royce on, 34; not a magical inheritance, 44 ff; has bodily conditions, 64 ff; has psychical conditions, 110 ff; in the sphere of the will, 177 ff; self-control fundamental to, 180 ff; problem of, of fixing attention, 191; objectivity a prime condition of, 192; work a chief means to, 198 ff; inner life source of, 237 ff; possibility of, implies that each person is an end in himself, 239; not to be compelled, 243; personal association a means to, 246 ff; persuasion a means to, 247; caught, not taught, 248.

Christ, the great Person, 192, 254; in Revelation, 245; built kingdom on ten men (association) 253 ff; actualizes ideal conditions for living, 256 ff; his teaching, 257 ff.

Christianity, not two kinds of, 96 ff; Harnack on, 97.

Classicism referred to, 222.

Clouston, Dr., on inhibitory power, 70.

Coe, referred to, 67; on modern conception of religious life, 235.

Coleridge, referred to, 233, 234.

Comparative psychology, 8.

Complexity of life, 3, 5 ff; does not mean confusion, 5; psychological grounds for, 7 ff.

Compromise, Lecky on, 39 ff.

Concreteness of the real, 210 ff, 220.

Conditions, only through fulfilment of, does man have power over nature, 39; Lecky's *Map of Life*, 39; underlie all great

achievement, 44; only in particulars, 45; but see Royce, 45 ff; need of pointing out exact conditions of life, 46 ff:
unity of man, first condition, 46; bodily, the basis of spiritual life, 48 ff, 64; bodily, not omnipotent, 79; psychical necessary, 110 ff; volitional necessary, 144 ff.

Consciousness, preceded by impulse to action, 147; naturally impulsive, 153; influence of practical interests in, 161 ff; all related, 211; fundamental convictions of, involved in emphasis upon concrete, 228.

Conservation of energy, and psychical states, 51 ff; James on, 52.

Convictions, fundamental, of supreme value, 128; practical interests in, 166 ff; of consciousness involved in concrete, 228; greatest, from personal associations, 250.

Corning, referred to, 65, 67, 72; rules for increasing nerve power, 82; on brain exhaustion, 83.

Cowles, Dr., on symptoms of fatigue, 72.

Dawson, interest of child in persons, 231.

Decision, 26; Tommy and Grizel, 27; Sully on, 27; Palmer on, 27 ff; should not be made in weak moment, 141.

Deland, Mrs., referred to, 242.

DeQuincy, referred to, 129.

Descartes, referred to, 125.

Dewey, referred to, 156; application of teleological principle, 164, 172; on society in terms of action, 174; genetic method, 219.

Discrimination, and assimilation, 24; of values in life, 29.

Diffusion, Law of, 55 ff.

Dilthey, on life and the notion, 213; referred to, 230.

Docility and initiative, Royce on, 33 ff.

Doubt, function of, provisional and temporary, 126.

Dresslar, referred to, 67.

Drudgery, Gannett on, 206 ff.

Drummond, referred to, 41; on character by association, 252.

Dualism, questioned, 53.

Du Bois, Patterson, referred to, 231, 236, 239; on fatherhood, 238; on personal relations as means to character, 248.

Dunn, Martha Baker, quoted, 152.

Duties, significance of, 42 ff.

Duty, the demands of, and bodily interests, 94 ff; Herrmann on, 184.

Dynamogenesis, law of, 150.

Ecce Homo, referred to, 189, 252.

Ecclesiastes, referred to, 169.

Education, valuable for endurance, 12; tested by number of interests, 13; Sully, Volkmann, and Royce on, 13; opportunities for will-training in, 88 ff; danger in, 127; protest needed in interest of whole man, 227 ff.

Educational counsel of our time, 256.

Elective system, abuse of, 134.

Eliot, George, referred to, on contagion of ideas, 252 ff.

Elijah, referred to, 202.

Emerson, referred to, 74.

Emotion, paradoxes in, 30; proper control of, 82, 187 ff; influence of, on body and mind, 135 ff; bearing of, on volition, 137 ff; danger of sham, 138 ff; healthful, not manufactured, 139; danger of passive, 141 ff; need of power to withstand strong, 142 ff; James on, 143; Jastrow on, 143; Höffding on, 144; controlled only through attention or action, 187; Höffding on control of, 188; Royce on, 188 ff; *Ecce Homo* on, 189; Spinoza, and Paul, as James quotes him, 189 ff; Dr. Chalmers, referred to, 190.

Emphases, psychological, current, 171 ff; on persons and personal relations, 228 ff.

Emphasis, psychological, on complexity of life, 5 ff; on paradox of life, 22 ff; on conditions, 39 ff; on central importance of will and action, 145 ff.

Empirical sciences, Windelband on, 224 ff

Encyclopedia Britannica, referred to, 211.

Ends and means, paradox in, 22.

Environment, not the entire, but what claims attention, makes man, 159.

Erdmann, on man as subject of modern philosophy, 8; referred to, 9; on paradox in religion, 31; on despotism of Frederick the Great, 243.

Essence, only meaning of, teleological, 162 ff.

Everett, against Neitsche, on friendship, 38; referred to, 251.

Exclusiveness, nowhere justified, 16 ff; history of philosophy against, 18.

Evolution, suggestion of, 146; definite setting forth of theory, 218.

Exercise, bodily, volitional as well as physical in effects, 59; need of wisdom in, 66 ff; Corning on, 67; LaGrange, quoted on, 67; Dr. Gulick on, 75; Herbert Spencer on, 75; value of "unnecessary," 99.

Experience, meaning of, 9; dependent on range of interests, 10; action the natural terminus of, 149 ff.

Experiences, terminate in action, 4; Royce on sensory, 104 ff; cannot be sought as ends, 140.

Experimental psychology, Külpe on, 2; defined, 8; Mosso in, 56; Henle in, 56 ff.

Experiments, of Mosso, 56; of Henle, 56 ff; of Du Bois Reymond, 57; of Dr. Sequin, 57; in New York State Reformatory, 58; of Corning, on circulation, 65; of Dr. Hodge on nerve-cells, 71.

Expression, necessary to life, 199.

Faith, physiological effect of, 83; Dr. George E. Gorham on, 83 ff; implied in willingness to use powers, 169.

Fatigue, a poisoning of the blood, 65; effects of, 67 ff; effect of, on nerve conditions, 70 ff; effects of, on perceptions and activities, 71 ff; Mosso on, 65, 66, 72; Dr. Cowles on symptoms of, 72; intellectually and morally dangerous, 73.

Fichte, referred to, 147, 172, 251; on vocation, 167; on respect for personality, 246.

Foster, John, on decision of character, 91.

Frederick the Great, referred to, 243.

Freedom, dependent on wide range of interests, 12; moral, of others, must be respected, 236 ff.

Fremantle, referred to, 20; quoted, 156.

French enlightenment, referred to, 18.

Friendship, significance of, according to Ritschl, 37; Everett against Neitsche on, 38; an important psychological motive, 231 ff; many a, hurt by lack of respect, 244.

Gannett, referred to, 43; on drudgery, 206 ff.

"Genius and old-fogyism," 25.

Goethe, referred to, 94, 195, 245; Carlyle's recognition of, 158; on theme of the world's history, 169.

Gorham, Dr. George E., on physiological effects of faith, 83 ff.

Granger, Augustine, quoted by, 123 ff; St. Teresa, on sham graces, 139; quoted, 244 ff.

Granville, Dr. J. M., on surplus nervous energy, 70; on nerve power as the force of life, 79; on brain work and worry, 83; on work, 203.

Growth, physical conditions of, 64 ff; psychical conditions of, 110 ff; in character, two theories of, 194 ff.

Gulick, on exercise, 75.

Habit, physical basis of, 61, 87; time-limit in, 61, 86; James on, 62, 85 ff; phenomena of, illustrate unity of body and mind, 85; significance of, for mental life, 86; in education, 88; James' maxims on, 90 ff; fixed by action alone, 92.

Habits, intellectual, as helps, 113 ff; as hindrances, 124 ff; of study, dangers in, 133.

Hale, Edward Everett, referred to, 81.

Hall, G. Stanley, on muscle-habits and will, 59; on physical culture in will training, 95; on danger in study of philosophy, 124; on need of living out theories, 129; on abuse of elective system, 134; on will and action, 145; on the body for action, 150 ff.

Hamilton, referred to, 19.

Happiness, bodily conditions of, 48 ff; psychical conditions of, 110 ff; in exercise of will, 178 ff; in endurance of hardship, Walter Wellman on, 178; Wundt and Lotze on, 178, 179, 180; self-control

INDEX

fundamental to, 182 ff; Hawthorne on, 185; objectivity, prime condition of, 192; love, greatest source of, 196; work a chief means to, 198 ff; not to be compelled, 243; personal association a means to, 246 ff.

Harnack, on true Christianity and asceticism, 97; on biography, 226.

Harris, Dr., referred to, 171 ff.

Haste, hurtful to brain power, 81 ff.

Hawthorne, on self-control and happiness, 185.

Health, in determining will, 80.

Hegel, referred to, 216, 221, 223; idea of organism in, 216 ff.

Helps, intellectual, 113.

Henle, experiments of, in psychology, 56 ff; on effect of joyful emotions, 135.

Herrick, Robert, *The Common Lot*, 205 ff.

Herrmann, on duty, 184.

"Heterogony of ends" (Wundt), 156.

Hilty, quoted, 201; on man created for activity, 202 ff.

Hindrances, intellectual, 124 ff.

Hobbes, referred to, 14.

Höffding, on unchanged mental state, 14; on physical and psychical, 54; on phenomena of inhibition, 68; on power of self-control in insane, 79 ff; on mental hygiene, 110; quotes Ideler, 141; on reason and emotion, 144; on action and will, 145; on volitional activity and consciousness, 147; on development of will and thought, 158; on self-control as positive virtue, 188 ff; on interaction of whole man, 200; on psychical individuality, 226.

Hoffman, on interest and attention, 159.

Hospitality, a fundamental psychological motive, 231 ff.

Howells, referred to, 126, 222.

Hume, referred to, 108.

Hypnotism, evidence for unity of mind and body, 63, 136.

"Idealism of work," a theory of growth in character, 195.

Ideler, Höffding quotes, 141.

"Ideo-motor action," the normal type, James on, 153.

Idiots, effect of physical training on, 57.

Imagination, proper training of, 24; a clear and definite, direct help to sane living, 120 ff; trained best in connection with conduct, 155.

Imitation, influence of, 148, 246 ff; Sully and James on, 247.

Individualism, revolt against, 108.

Individuality, psychical, Höffding on, 226; of persons to be respected, 236 ff; of races, 242 ff; respect for, test of civilization, 245 ff.

Infancy, witness of, that man is made for personal relations, 230 ff.

Inferences, four great, from modern psychology, 1, 3, 4:
first, complexity of life, 5 ff; second, the unity of man, 47 ff; third, the central importance of will and action, 145 ff; fourth, the concreteness of the real, 210 ff.

Influence, dependent on wide range of interests, 11; breadth and depth of, dependent on sympathy with race-interests, 11, 12; conditions of, must be fulfilled to gain power, 17; paradox in, 30; of body on mind, 64 ff; of mind on body, 78 ff; psychical conditions of, implied in unity of mind, 103 ff; bearing of will on, 177 ff; self-control fundamental to, 185 ff; objectivity, prime condition of, 192, 197; work, a chief means to, 198 ff; of a person, 214; stronger than command, 237 ff; personal association, a means to, 246 ff; to be strong involves being at one's best, 255.

Inheritance, the best things not a magical, 44 ff.

Inhibition, dependent on fullness of life, 68; Höffding on phenomenon of, 68; Dr. Clouston on, 70; Dr. J. M. Granville on, 70; Dr. W. H. Burnham on, 70; rule of, 188.

Initiative, 33 ff; of the mind in habit, 61, 91.

Insanity, many forms of, not due to organic lesions, 65; Corning, Mosso, and LaGrange on, due to lack of self-control, 69; hence to loss of power of attention, 161,

INDEX

Intellect, fundamental function of, the discernment of relationships, 105 ff; discerns temperament, 115 ff; discerns what moral progress is, 118; need to keep clear and strong, 120 ff.

Intellectual hindrances, 124 ff.

Intellectual life, paradoxes in, 24 ff; Sully and Aristotle on habits in, 24; discrimination and assimilation, 24; the constant struggle between "genius and old-fogyism," 25.

Intellectual vagueness, immoral, 121; Lotze on, 122 ff; the chief danger in many forms of temptation, 130.

Interdependence of things, 42 ff; of mind and body, 47 ff; of intellectual functions, 103 ff; of intellect, feeling, and will, 106 ff; Royce on, 107, 210 ff.

Interests, wide range of, needed, 9, 114; reason for, 9 ff; experience dependent on, 10; influence dependent on, 11; freedom dependent on, 12; sanity dependent on, 12; chief test of one's education, 13; permanent, Sully on need of arousing, 13; Volkmann on, 13; Royce on, 13; human nature avenges lack of regard for, 15 ff; illustrations of need of, 16; religious life dependent on, 17 ff; absorption in the lower, defeats itself, 20; bodily, and the demands of duty, 94 ff; chief aim of education to enlarge circle of, 114; practical influence of, in consciousness, 161 ff; James on, 162; determines our modes of conceiving and naming things, 162; influence of, in reasoning, 163; in philosophical solutions, 163.

Introspection, to be guarded, 196.

James, on "reinstatement of the vague," 6, 211; on the dependence of experience on interest, 10; on "genius and old-fogyism," 25; on choice of lifework and character, 32; on independent reality of spiritual life, 50; statement of Bain's law of diffusion, 55; on muscular activity and will, 60; on time-limit of habits, 62; referred to, 77, 80, 108, 160, 225, 242; on the significance of habit for the mental life, 86 ff; maxims on habit, 90 ff; theory of emotions, 137; on reason and emotion, 143; on neural organism a machine for action, 150; on cognition, 153; on attention, 161; on influence of practical interests, 162; on powers of man, 168 ff; emphasis, on "selective" attention, 171; on place of will and action in life, 176; on war between abstract and concrete, 212; on tweedle-dum and tweedle-dee, 213; "pragmatism," 219; on imitation, 247; on convictions from association with others, 250.

Jastrow, Professor, on bodily conditions as a means of accomplishing our ends, 78; on reason and emotion, 143.

Job, referred to, 169.

Jordan, President, on revivals, 181.

Kant, referred to, 160, 216, 239, 251; Paulsen on, 167.

Keats, on axioms, 138; referred to, 155.

Kedney, referred to, 156.

Kekule, referred to, 214.

King, H. C., on self-assertion in character, 35; on bearing of emotion on volition, 137; referred to, 143, 235, 236, 242, 249, 250.

King, Irving, referred to, 219.

Kingsley, referred to, 81.

Kipling, referred to, 205.

Knowledge, of self, prime condition of growth, 114.

Külpe, on experimental psychology, 2; referred to, 6.

Laboratory, first psychological, 1.

Laboratory method justified, 156.

LaGrange, emphasis on quality of blood, 65; quoted on the gain of exercise, 65; on the need of wisdom in exercise, 67; on Sydenham, 76.

Lamb, Charles, Birrell on, 233 ff.

Law, prevails in physical, moral, and spiritual spheres, 41; Drummond's contribution concerning, 41; results conditioned on fulfilment of, 41.

Law of Diffusion, point of connection between psychical and physical, 55; James' statement of Bain's, 55; facts of, prove need of good blood, 65.

INDEX

Lecky, on paradox in character, 35 ff; on paradox in general conduct of life, 37; *The Map of Life*, 39 ff; referred to, 79, 200; on need of action in adolescence, 151; on education of the will, 177; on interest in others, 196.

Leisure, fruitful, the result of earnest work, and important, 208.

Life, complexity of, 3, 5 ff:

greater richness thereby, 5; psychological grounds for recognition of, 7 ff.

measured by range of interests, 9 ff; paradoxes of, 22 ff; conditions of, 39 ff; bodily, 48 ff; Professor James on, 86; enormous place of will and action in, 176 ff.

Life, religious, and asceticism, 93 ff.

Life, spiritual, requires fight against love of ease, 101; has intellectual, emotional, and volitional conditions, 112; means more than right convictions, 129.

Life-work and character, paradox in choice of, 31; James on, 32.

Literature and art, present themes concretely, 214 ff; development of, 222 ff.

Living, sane, intellectual conditions of, 113 ff; emotional conditions of, 135 ff; secret of staying in presence of the best, 192, 198; three great conditions of, 256; three great means of, 256.

Lotze, on need of relating and comparing, 15; thesis, to show significance of mechanism, 23; on significance of work and duties, 43; referred to, 107; on mind's "vision of unity," 108 ff; on intellectual vagueness, 122 ff; on danger in study of philosophy, 125; on danger in vagueness, 131 ff; on rank of human body, 152; on the practical, in convictions, 166; on contribution of effort to happiness, 179; on theory of self-development, 195; on concreteness of the whole man, 227; on relations, 229.

Love, the all-inclusive virtue, 196; Christ's teaching summed up in self-sacrificing, 258.

Lowell, quoted, 43; referred to, 132.

Luther, referred to, 112.

Man, a unity:

the subject of modern psychology, 8; as sum of all, 8; brought out by physiological psychology, 47 ff;

distinctive mark of, power of "prevision," 180; characterized by power of self-control, 180; created for activity, 202 ff; whole revealed only in personal relations, 233 ff.

Mansell, referred to, 19.

Martineau, referred to, 177.

Materialism, not the end of modern science, 49, 51; Paulsen referred to, 51.

Matheson, Dr., on obedience of the child, 238.

Maurice, referred to, 234.

Maxims, James', on habit, 90 ff.

Mechanism, necessary but not the end, 22; means and ends must be harmonized, 23; Lotze, on position of, 23.

Memories, kind of, important, 117; clear and definite, a most direct intellectual help to right living, 120.

Mill, John Stuart, referred to, 194.

Mind, influenced by body, 64; search of, for unity, 108 ff; organized for action, 153 ff; made for relations, 213 ff.

Modern philosophy, its subject man, 8; reflects the Reformation, 8; a protest against denial of complexity of life, 9.

Moods, influence of, on willing, 140.

Mosso, experiments in psychology, 56; on phenomena of fatigue, 65, 66, 72 ff; on need of nerve power in attention, 67; Dr. Chamberlain on, referred to, 67; on attention, 69.

Müller, Max, referred to, 250.

Munger, Dr., referred to, 75.

Münsterberg, referred to, 160, 211; on life in terms of the will, 172 ff, 177; protest for whole man, 221 ff; on science and psychology, 225; on character by association, 253.

Mysticism, ignoring of the particular, a great error of, 45; real truth in, 234.

Mystics of the seventeenth century referred to, 18.

INDEX

Natural science, lessons of, 40 ff; as to need of understanding conditions, 41 ff; as to connection of spiritual life with bodily conditions, 48 ff; methods of, and of history, approaching each other, 224, 226.

Naturalism, inconsistent, 53.

Nervous energy, a necessity in attention, 67; Corning's rules for meeting special conditions of, 82; necessity of proper control of emotions, 82 ff; development of, in education, 89.

Nervous system in forming habits, 61.

Neural organism, a machine for action, 150.

Neurasthenia, an American disease, 76.

Neitsche, referred to, 38.

Oberlin, referred to, 16.

Objectivity, a prime condition of character, happiness, and influence, 192 ff.

"Old-fogyism," 25.

Organism, influence of idea of, in history of thought, 215 ff; before Hegel, 216; in Hegel, 216 ff; since Hegel, 218 ff; analogy of, inadequate, 223 ff.

Over-activity of Americans, 209.

Palmer, Professor, on decision, 27 ff.

Paradoxes of life, 22 ff; of ends and means, 22; of different spheres of life, 23 ff; physical, 23; intellectual, 24 ff; Sully on, 26; moral, 26 ff;
decision, 26; enthusiasm and quietism, 28;
of true simplicity, 29; of emotion, 30: in influence, 30; in religion, 31; Erdmann on, 31; in choice of life-work and character, 31 ff; James on, 32; fundamental, involved in very natures, 33; docility and initiative, Royce on, 33 ff; King on, 35; Lecky on, 35; in general conduct of life, 36 ff; Lecky on, 37; Ritschl on, 37; Everett against Neitsche, on, 38; Biedermann on, 38; psychology's emphasis on, means emphasis on conditions, 38.

Pascal, referred to, 165.

Pathological psychology, 7.

Paul, on true asceticism, 99 ff; referred to, 112; referred to and quoted by Professor James, 189 ff; comparison of Church to a body, 216; on training of children, 242 ff.

Paulsen, referred to, 51, 129, 146, 147, 178, 248; on danger in vagueness of thought, 132; on the practical in conviction, 166; on Kant, 167.

Peary, on value of education for endurance, 12.

Person, recognition of sacredness of, 239 ff; this the highest test of civilization, 245 ff.

Personality, of others, respect for, 236 ff; respect for, highest test of civilization, 245 ff.

Personal relations, more than organic, 224; psychological emphasis on, 228; bodies made for, 230; witness of infancy that man is made for, 230; witness of moral history of the race to need of, 231 ff; witness of philosophy to need of, 232; whole man revealed only in, 233; power of, 246 ff; men made for, 248; the greatest means to character, 249 ff.

Persons, psychological emphasis on, 228 ff; interest of infancy and childhood in, 230 ff; respect for moral freedom of, 236 ff.

Philosophy, only solution of problems of, practical, 165; witness of, to need of personal relations, 232 ff.

Physical, paradoxes in realm of, 23; close connection of, with spiritual, 48 ff; this proved by law of diffusion; James' statement of this law, 55.

Physical training, effects of, on mind, 57; need of, for higher life, 77; Sully quoted on, 77; James referred to, on, 77; exercise and will, 58; Sully on, 58 ff; G. Stanley Hall on, 59; Dr. Maclaren's inquiries on, 59.

Physiological psychology, defined, 7; mission to show unity of man, 47 ff; on the phenomena of fatigue, 69.

Pfleiderer, on asceticism, 98.

Plato, referred to, 144.

Plus-health, need of, 75.

Pope, referred to, 216.

Practical, the, in consciousness, 162 ff; in conception and reasoning, 162 ff; in philosophical solutions, 163 ff; in convictions, 166 ff; Job's problem also in Ecclesiastes, 169 ff; among Christian university students in Berlin, 170.

Pragmatism, 219 ff.

Prevision, distinctive mark of man, 180.

Problems, theoretical solution of, impossible, 168 ff; see Job and Ecclesiastes, 169 ff; of university students in Berlin, 170.

Protest, in interest of whole man continually needed, 220 ff; in history of literature, 222 ff; in philosophy, 223 ff; in history, 224 ff; in education, 227 ff.

Psychology, emphasis of modern, upon experimental side, 2; meaning of the movement, 2 ff; Royce on, and Külpe, 2; four great inferences from, 3.

First emphasis upon complexity of life, 5 ff: physiological, defined, 7; race, 7; pathological, 7; comparative, 8; experimental method in, 8; declares need of wide range of interests, 9 ff; emphasizes the relatedness of all, 14 ff; sees the paradoxes of life, 22 ff; emphasizes the conditions of life, 39 ff.

Second emphasis upon unity of man, 47 ff; evidence for unity of mind and body, 55 ff; unity of the mind, 103 ff; affirms one fundamental function of mind, 105; interdependence also of intellect, feeling, and will, 106 ff.

Third emphasis upon central importance of will and action, 145 ff; current emphasis of, 171 ff.

Fourth great emphasis on, the concreteness of the real, 210 ff.

Puritanism, the new, 93.

Purpose, right, broad application of, 118; deep application of, 119; skilful and delicate application of, 120; born of conviction, 138.

Quo Vadis (Chilo), referred to, 123.

Race psychology, defined, 7.

Raphael's Sistine Madonna, 193.

Rational living, bodily conditions of, 48 ff; based on good blood, 65; Dr. Trumbull on, 80; the law of habit in, 87; intellectual conditions of, 110 ff; volitional conditions of, 144 ff; three great conditions of, 256; three great means of, 256.

Real, the, is concrete, 3, 210 ff; cannot be abstractly defined, 211 ff, 220.

Realism, referred to, 222, 235.

"Realism of self-development," a theory of growth in character, 194.

Reality, emotion adds greatly to sense of, 135 ff; only standard of, within us, 165.

Reason, need to exercise in case of exciting emotion, 143; James on, 143; Höffding on, 144.

Reformation, the, reflected in modern philosophy, 8.

Reformatory, New York State, experiments in, 58.

Relatedness of all, 14 ff; recognition of, required to give value to interest, 65; recognition of, carries denial of possible separation of sacred and secular, 17, 42 ff; not opposed to personality, 229.

Relating, need of, for complete knowledge, 15.

Relations, multiplicity and intricacy of, 5 ff.

Relativity of human knowledge, 19.

Religion, paradoxes in, and Erdmann on, 31; Biedermann on, 38; not a magical inheritance, 44; is life, 186.

Religious life, and asceticism, 93 ff; self-control a necessity, 180 ff; Coe on modern conception of, 235.

Religious movements of our time, 19.

Respect for liberty and personality of others, 236 ff.

Results, conditioned on fulfilment of law, 41.

Revivals, President Jordan on, 181; involve reason and self-control, 181.

Reymond, Du Bois, on psychology of physical exercises, 57.

Richardson, referred to, 83.

Ritschl, on significance of friendship, 37; on manufactured emotions, 139 ff.

Romanes, on value of emotions, 136 ff.

Romanticism, referred to, 222.

Romanticists, referred to, 185.

INDEX

Royce, on the scope of psychology, 2; on need of arousing permanent interests, 13 ff; classification of mental phenomena, 33 ff; on self-assertion and self-surrender, 34 ff; on tendency to fixed habit of mind, 45 ff; on time-limit in habits, 62; referred to, 72, 171, 246; on interdependence of mental powers, 104 ff; on unity of intellectual and voluntary powers, 107; on philosophy, 125; on impulse to imitative action, 148 ff; on training of imagination, 155; rule of inhibition, 188 ff; on thinking as a kind of living, 217; on human instinct for association, 230 ff.

Ruskin, quoted by Miss Call, 82.

Sacred and secular, denial of separation of, 17.
Sanity, dependent on wide range of interests, 12.
Schelling, referred to, 216.
Schlegel, and the Romanticists, 185.
Sciences, empirical, 224 ff.
Schleiermacher, referred to, 216.
Schopenhauer, referred to, 147, 193.
Seeley, referred to, 158; *Ecce Homo*, contagion of character, 252.
Self, knowledge of, a prime condition of growth, 114 ff; consciousness possible only through volition, 147; imitative activity the bridge between earlier and later stages of, 148; the social, 228 ff.
Self-control, effect of fatigue on, 67 ff; a basis of character, 68 ff, 74; power of, dependent on attention, 69, 74; made easier by right bodily conditions, 79; power of, in insane, Höffding on, 79; as to emotions, 82 ff; Richardson on, 83; volitional, 83; Dr. George E. Gorham on control of emotions, 83 ff, 187 ff; bodily functions affected by, 85; positive character of, 85, 96, 183 ff, 187 ff; looks to growth, 95 ff; Paul on the need of, 99 ff; attention at basis of, 161; fundamental character of, 180 ff:
to moral and religious character, 180; to happiness, 182; to influence, 185.
Self-denial, combined with self-assertion, 32; Royce on, 34; King on, 35; Lecky on, 35; value of, in formation of character, 92, 93; in unnecessary things, 97 ff; the true value of, 98.
Self-development, theory of, fundamentally deficient, 195 ff.
Sequin, Dr., in training of idiots, 57.
Shaftsbury, idea of organism, 216.
Shah of Persia, interest in Derby, referred to, 212 ff.
Sheppard, Nathan, referred to, 92.
Sill, E. R., quoted, 45.
Simplicity, true, demands of, 29.
Smiles, referred to, 160.
Socrates, referred to, 112.
Spencer, Herbert, referred to, 75.
Spinoza, referred to, 189.
Spiritual life, close connection of, with physical, 48 ff; not materialistic, 49 ff; James on independence of, 50, 52 ff; and the "passion for material comfort," 101; may not ignore power of emotions, 138.
Spheres of life, paradoxes in different, 23 ff.
St. John, referred to, 20.
St. Teresa, referred to through Granger, 139.
Starr, quoted, 65; on lack of self-control, 69; on imperfect educational methods, 103 ff.
Stephen, Leslie, referred to, 222.
Stephenson, referred to, 126, 205.
Study, proper kind of, 134 ff.
Sully, on need of arousing permanent interests, 13; on best mental habits, 24; on decision, 27; on nervous and mental processes, 54; on connection of will and muscular activity, 58 ff; on need of physical training, 77; on unity of mind, 104; on discipline, 237; on imitation, 247.
Sydenham, mentioned, 76.
Symbolism, referred to, 222.

Temperament, knowledge of, essential, 115 ff; as to powers, 116 ff; as to memories, 117.
Temptation, a chief danger in, from intellectual vagueness, 130 ff; Lotze on 130.
Thinking, relation of, to right living, 113.
Tolstoi, referred to, 126, 205.

INDEX

Training, all real, of whole man, body, mind, and spirit, 61; of the will, in physical culture, 95.

Trumbull, Dr., referred to, 80.

Unity of man, 3.

Unity of body and mind, 47 ff; recognized in asceticism, 47 ff; psychological evidence for, 55 ff; suggestions for living from, 64 ff.

Unity of mind, 103 ff; intellectual functions interdependent, 103 ff; intellect, feeling, and will also interdependent, 106 ff; shown by search of mind for unity, 108; suggestions for living from, 111 ff; implies certain conditions, 112 ff: intellectual, 113 ff; emotional, 135 ff; volitional, 144 ff.

Vague, the, James on reinstatement of, 6.

Vagueness, intellectual, immoral, 121; gives chief danger to temptation, 130 ff.

Volition, bearing of emotion on, 137 ff; of moods on, 140 ff.

Volitional self-control, 83.

Volkmann, on need of arousing permanent interests, 13.

Wagner, "Venus music," referred to, 132.

Wagner, Charles, quoted on negations, 127.

Wakefulness, degrees of, 14.

Ward, quoted, 53.

Ward, Mrs., referred to, 16.

Weariness, a warning against over-activity, 71.

Wellman, Walter, on pleasure in endurance, 178 ff.

Westcott, Bishop, on asceticism, 101.

Wiggin, Mrs., quoted, 194.

Will, and action, of central importance, 3, 145 ff; muscular activity and, 58 ff; Stanley Hall on, 59; in determining conditions of health, 80; in achieving rest, 80; volitional self-control, 83; training of, in education, 88 ff; power of attention the center of, 90; influence of moods on, 140 ff; development of, affects thought, 158; in attention, 159 ff; freedom of, in attention, 160; enormous place of, in life, 176 ff; effort of, contributes to happiness, 178 ff.

Will-training, Stanley Hall on, 95; ample field for, in requirements of health, 100 ff; most vital of all problems, 177.

Windelband, on the empirical sciences, 224 ff, 226.

Work, significance of, 42; small matters may not be slighted, 42; Lotze on, 43; Lowell on, 43; Gannett on, 43; Bishop of Exeter on, 43; effect of mental, upon nerve cells, 71; upon things, as protection against sophistry, 126; chief means to character, happiness, and influence, 198 ff; real, requires purpose, 201; one of the profoundest needs of man's nature, 203; means simply the common task, 204 ff; fruits in right leisure, 208 ff.

Wundt, *Outlines of Physiological Psychology*, referred to, 1, 168; "heterogony of ends," 156 ff; on civilization, 159; on the practical in convictions, 166 ff; on play, 178; on contribution of will and action to happiness, 179; on rules of good manners, 199; on conception of work, 203 ff; on poetic quality of modern life, 205; on reality, 212; on humoristic spirit, 231 ff.

Yonge, Miss, quoted, 241.

Zeller, referred to, 89, 182.